I believe there's a ti[me] [to visit] Singapore, this is that time. You may have heard of its strict reputation and ban on chewing gum, but the Singapore I know is more than just a clean, safe place. It's also friendly, and most of all, delightfully multi-faceted.

Whether you're exploring the bustling markets and colorful streets of Little India, the hipster enclave of Tiong Bahru, Chinatown's smoky temples and dim sum houses, or the carpet bazaars and tea parlors of the Arab Quarter, there's something truly magical happening here.

What you hold in your hands is a guide to the Singapore you won't read about elsewhere – an introduction to the personalities and stories behind this food and fashion mecca that's bursting with hidden finds (you just need to know where to look).

the hunt singapore editors

bernie baskin

Bernie Baskin is an eternal wanderer who fell in love with Singapore's back alleys and culinary marvels more than five years ago. When he's not dreaming up the perfect itinerary for his next adventure, he can be found on the back of his vintage motorcycle, hunting for the hidden, the authentic, the unique, the gems.

jalean wong

An unabashed lover of food in all its amazing forms, Singapore native Jalean Wong has spent her life searching for the world's tastiest (sometimes spiciest) nosh, both as a professional food critic and for her own unadulterated personal pleasure. Although this equal opportunity eater's palate has been finely honed while living in the US, Australia and China, she is just as content scouting out hole-in-the-walls as she is stuffing her face with a 10-course degustation.

here to lay
ry head

HOTEL FORT CANNING

Colonial appeal in lush surroundings

11 Canning Walk Singapore S(178881) / +65 6559 6770 / hfcsingapore.com

Deluxe double from $350

One of the things I love most about Singapore's tropical climate – and it sure as hell isn't the humidity – is how much greenery abounds. If, like me, that appeals to you, then this 86-room boutique hotel is the place to stay when you next visit. You'll be hard pressed to find a more charming spot in such a luxuriantly green setting. What was once a base for the British in World War II has been restored with a modern, minimal aesthetic, complete with 14th century artifacts for good measure.

NEW MAJESTIC HOTEL

Heritage chic in Chinatown

31-37 Bukit Pasoh Road S(089845) / +65 65792026 / newmajestichotel.com

Standard double from $250

Tucked away on a side street in Chinatown is the 30-room "heritage chic" New Majestic. The boutique hotel is a fusion of all things old and new. Individually designed rooms may feature six meter high ceilings (the attic suites), vintage furniture, personal gardens or freestanding copper bathtubs in the bathroom. On the ground floor, beneath the outdoor pool, is Majestic Restaurant (see page 13) – a beacon of inspired Cantonese cuisine.

ST. REGIS

Unadulterated luxury near Orchard Road

29 Tanglin Rd S(247911) / +65 6506 6888 / stregissingapore.com

Executive deluxe double from $900

If plush elegance and luxurious opulence are what you're seeking, please allow me to unequivocally recommend the St. Regis. From the jaw dropping breakfast spread and masterful artwork to the richly appointed suites and pampering spa treatments at Remède – well, five stars may just not be enough. The hotel is also ideally located – the Singapore Botanic Gardens are a 10-minute walk away or, if you'd prefer to stretch the plastic rather than your legs, 10 minutes on foot in the opposite direction will get you to Orchard Road (see page 62).

THE SULTAN

Real Singapore charm in the Arab Quarter

101 Jalan Sultan S(199002) / +65 6723 7101 / thesultan.com.sg

Platform double from $175

I fell in love with the Kampong Glam neighborhood the first time I wandered through her twisting alleys and sat at her sidewalk cafes to smoke shisha, sip mint tea and nibble honeyed baklava. The Sultan sits comfortably within the area's mélange of culture, rich history and delicious culinary experiences. This inviting 64-room boutique hotel is the product of a faithful, loving restoration of 10 conservation shophouses with unique architectural features.

WANDERLUST

Eccentric haven in Little India

2 Dickson Road S(209494) / +65 6396 3322 / wanderlusthotel.com

Standard double from $200

The funky Wanderlust is a 29-room boutique hotel located in the heart of Little India. The interior, to put it mildly, is eclectic, borne from a collaboration between four of Singapore's finest design agencies. The aesthetic melds an industrial glam lobby with minimalistic black and white rooms and eccentric neon-lit chambers. There's something here for the design freak in us all. And of course, this being Singapore, there's a top-notch restaurant on hand to sate those hunger pangs – Cocotte is an award winning rustic French restaurant that dishes up hearty meaty portions and fresh crusty breads).

chinatown

ann siang

Just one visit to Chinatown is enough to dispel
the image of Singapore being a clean city
populated only by law-abiding citizens. People
jaywalk, there are touts and knockoffs galore,
and you'll even – shock – find scattered rubbish!
That said, few neighborhoods are as close
to my heart. The lively – almost to a fault at
times – mishmash of heritage spots alongside a
veritable assortment of old school and spanking
new eateries is a combination that's hard to
resist. Head to Ann Siang, now bursting with
trendy boutiques and lovely restaurants, which
intersects Club Street, the unofficial center for
the boisterous expat bar scene.

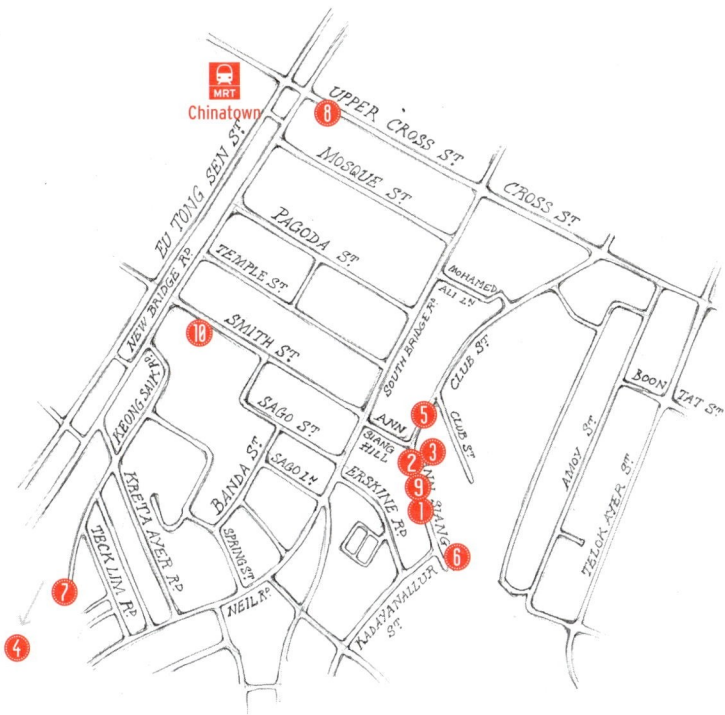

1   Finespun Clothiers
2   Goto Japanese Restaurant
3   Kki Sweets Cafe - the little dröm store
4   Majestic Restaurant (off map)
5   MYthology

6   PS. Cafe
7   Rose Citron
8   Spring Court Restaurant
9   Swagger
10 The Good Beer Company

FINESPUN CLOTHIERS

Bespoke menswear

28 Ann Siang Road S(069708) / **+65 6225 6016** / finespunclothiers.com

Back in the day I fancied myself a dapper dresser and I confess to still being a bit of a dandy. No surprise then that I adore Finespun Clothiers and its lovely owner/designer Caroline Yak. Not only does Caroline have an astounding eye for design, she is also incredibly helpful at enlightening men on how to build a proper wardrobe (advice I could have used in my early peacocking days). Caroline comes from a family with deep haberdashery roots and is the perfect person to bring your wardrobe dreams to life. She also carries her own line of dress shirts and custom shoes for those seeking a touch of style on the fly.

GOTO JAPANESE RESTAURANT

Exquisite kaiseki

#01-01, 14 Ann Siang Road S(069694) / +65 6438 1553

I've been asked countless times what my all-time favorite cuisine is. I must confess I don't really have one, but Japanese is definitely up there. A real standout is this elegant 20-seater run by husband and wife team Hisao and Saori Goto. Saori, always graceful in a kimono, runs front of house while Hisao aka Goto-san crafts beautiful dishes with ingredients imported from Japan. We're talking serious caliber – Goto-san used to be an ex-Japanese ambassador's personal chef – and serious coin for prix fixe menus. A nine-course dinner will set you back $180 and the six-course lunch goes for $68, but worth every cent in my honest opinion.

KKI SWEETS CAFE -
THE LITTLE DRÖM STORE

Pâtisserie and toy store

7 Ann Siang Hill S(069791) / +65 6225 6650
kki-sweets.com / thelittledromstore.com

Give me a boutique pâtisserie coupled with a children's toy store and I'm in
heaven. I know I'm not five, but I don't mind acting it now and then. (Why
is my female editor smiling?) This hangout is a bit hidden, but the pastries
are worth the hunt. The crowd may be a bit young, but listen to the latest
teenage gossip and you might learn something to up your street cred. Just
beside the pâtisserie is The Little Dröm Store, run by the bubbly Antoinette.
Her shop is filled with toy cameras, costume jewelry and other cutsie gifts
that cater to the crowd that gathers here for afternoon coffee.

MAJESTIC RESTAURANT

Modern Cantonese cuisine

Ground Floor New Majestic Hotel, 31-37 Bukit Pasoh Road S(089845)
+65 6511 4718 / restaurantmajestic.com

Cantonese is generally considered the most refined of all Chinese cuisine and the folks at Majestic Restaurant go all out to ensure that their food lives up to the hype – and then some. Playfully located underneath the Majestic Hotel's swimming pool, the restaurant offers outstanding dim sum (à la traditional Cantonese), but it's the dinner menu that entices me. Chef-owner Yong Bing Ngen (well known in Singaporean culinary circles) has developed a wow-worthy menu with highlights such as perfectly steamed, fresh Boston lobster and tender stewed noodles, plated on beautiful blue-and-white porcelain. One visit my friend, and takeaway will never sully your lips again.

MYTHOLOGY

Frock-tastic boudoir

88 Club Street S(069456) / +65 6223 5570 / my-thology.com

Ladies, whenever a wedding invitation arrives, does frock panic immediately set in? Or have you ever wondered where to get your hands on an elegant, demure dress suitable for the British countryside? Or a va-va-voom gown for that Italian palazzo bash? Allow me to introduce you to MYthology. Owner and stylista supreme Apsara has created the ultimate platform for up and coming Asian designers, focusing mainly on dresses, but also boasting sassy separates and bold baubles. Style-wise, think ethnic inspired with ornate beading on fine silks, flowing chiffon in bright hues, and avant-garde silhouettes. In a nutshell? One-of-a-kind outfits to dazzle, whatever the occasion.

PS. CAFE

American and European favorites

#02-02, 45 Ann Siang Road S(069719)
+65 9797 0648 / pscafe.sg/ann-siang-hill

There are few places I'd rather lounge in than a gloriously presented European bistro. The folks behind PS. Cafe have outdone themselves with their three story, lushly imagined Ann Siang Hill hideaway. Enormous bouquets of foliage and flowers greet diners at every step. The stylish inside dining area is on the second floor, where the green theme continues with beautiful but subtle floral tabletop arrangements. However, the stunner is without doubt the exposed-brick courtyard rooftop with a view over the charming Chinatown shophouses. Nighttime brings many surprises, including a remarkably lively Friday night cocktail crowd downing locally inspired drinks such as the vodka cheng teng.

ROSE CITRON

Bright, colorful furnishings and clothing

23 Keong Saik Road S(089130)
+65 6323 1368 / rosecitron.com.sg

Rose Citron is a perfect name for this colorful, upbeat boutique in the heart of Chinatown. Owner Zoe Borie (a French expat who's been in Asia for many years) designs all the vibrant floral bags, children's clothing and jewelry in-house. Her zesty cushion collection is a personal favorite. Toss two lime hippo cushions on a vintage wooden bench and shabam! Nothing says modern style like this warm combination of old wood and vibrant colors. For the children, RC carries a darling collection of tiny sundresses and soft toys. If like mine, your abode could use a little sunshine, RC is where you'll find it.

SPRING COURT RESTAURANT

Oldest Chinese restaurant in Singapore

52-66 Upper Cross Street S(058348)
+65 6449 5030 / springcourt.com.sg

Spring Court Restaurant is the oldest family run Chinese restaurant in town (since 1929). These days, it's well known for traditional Chinese fine dining, so you're likely to see ladies wearing their colorful cheongsams to dinner. The menu is filled with authentic family recipes such as the humble Fujian style popiah. Although a typical street hawker dish, the recipe here comes from Ms. Soon's mother, who used to prepare it for her family each Chinese New Year. Their richly aromatic Peking-style duck is addictive. So throw on your cheongsam ladies, and treat yourselves.

SWAGGER

A gentleman's accouterment and style house

15 Ann Siang Road S(069695) / **+65 62235880** / swaggerstore.co

I remember my first wander through Swagger. It was a hot day (surprise) and I was sweating profusely. I was praying for shade when I passed a window showcasing classic men's shaving kits. Curious, I nudged open the door only to be hit by the rich smell of leather and fine cologne...and air conditioning. I swept through into the store, eyes agog at the array of cufflinks and pocketsquares, tweed jackets and leather satchels before me. I lifted my eyes to the salesman who had appeared bearing a glass of iced water. "I can make it a whiskey if you'd prefer," he crooned. My kind of place.

THE GOOD BEER COMPANY

Wicked craft brews

#02-58 Chinatown Complex, 335 Smith Street S(051335)
+65 9430 2750 / facebook.com/goodbeersg

Owner Daniel Goh gave into his love of suds and let's just say I'm not the only one who's glad he did. The result's a modest hawker stall stocking over 50 ciders and beers from Asia, Europe and the US. Sample a range of goods like UK's Wychwood Hobgoblin, Stone Oaked Arrogant Bastard Ale (USA), Echigo Pilsner from Japan as well as Kiasu Stout, care of Singapore's own Jungle Beer. The best bit? There are dozens of hawker dishes available including claypot rice and sambal stingray from nearby stalls to pair with your poison. You don't have to be a hardcore enthusiast to appreciate the beauty of that.

CHICKEN RICE

the lion city's best
hawker centers

Authentic local street food

EAST COAST LAGOON FOOD CENTRE
1220 East Coast Parkway, East Coast Park S(468960)

MAXWELL ROAD HAWKER CENTRE
1 Kadayanallur Street S(069184)

OLD AIRPORT ROAD FOOD CENTRE
Block 51 Old Airport Road S(390051)

171A
SATAY

When I'm in the mood for an epic *Man v. Food*-esque chow down, I head straight for the mother of all hawker centers: **Old Airport Road Food Centre**. Open from early morning to late at night, this place is huge. But it's not just the sheer size of it that impresses – the variety and quality of the grub is also top-notch. Just ask the throngs of diners who filter through here all day long. For us, evening is the best time to experience this beast. Grab a Tiger beer and take your time choosing what you want to eat from places like Mattar Road Seafood Barbecue (#01-63) for delectable chili crab, Cho Kee Noodle (#01-04) for wanton noodles, Lao Fu Zi Fried Kway Teow (#01-12) for delicious but seriously calorific flat rice noodles and Nam Sing Hokkien Fried Mee (#01-32) for fried Hokkien noodles. Better yet, order them all!

If you want to stay in the city, head to **Maxwell Road Hawker Centre** – a food pilgrimage site visited by chefs such as Anthony Bourdain and Gordon Ramsay. Not to be missed is Maxwell Fuzhou Oyster Cake (#01-05), a family-run spot that has been pumping out tasty golden fried oyster cakes – always better smothered in chili sauce – for over 50 years. Other picks include Tian Tian Hainanese Chicken Rice (#01-10/11), Zhen Zhen Porridge (#01-54) and Lim Kee Banana Fritters (#01-61) for some of the crispiest, sweetest banana fritters on the island. I bet that you'll be back for seconds.

Finally, another place for Singaporean specialties with a somewhat more romantic setting is **East Coast Lagoon Food Centre**. This seaside hawker center boasts fantastic stalls including Roxy Laksa (#01-48) for dependable Katong laksa, Song Kee Fried Oyster (#01-15) for or *luak* (oyster omelet), Haron 30 Satay (#01-55) for barbecued chicken and mutton skewers, Leng Heng Seafood BBQ (#01-06) for sambal (chili) stingray and Ah Hwee BBQ (#01-14) for BBQ chicken wings. After eating your fill, ease your guilty conscience by taking a stroll down the beach at East Coast Park.

tanjong pagar

duxton hill

Tanjong Pagar is one of the most charming areas of the city. A wonderful balance of traditional and modern elements, the skyscrapers juxtaposed against historic landmarks such as temples, mosques and churches make for a striking backdrop. Quaint, cobblestoned Duxton Hill, overrun by dodgy KTV bars just a few years ago (some of these girlie bars have survived the government's attempts to clean up the area), now lays claim to a glut of dining options to be found in repurposed conservation shophouses. For those so inclined, this is also a rainbow-friendly area with popular nightspots dotted along Neil Road and Tanjong Pagar Road.

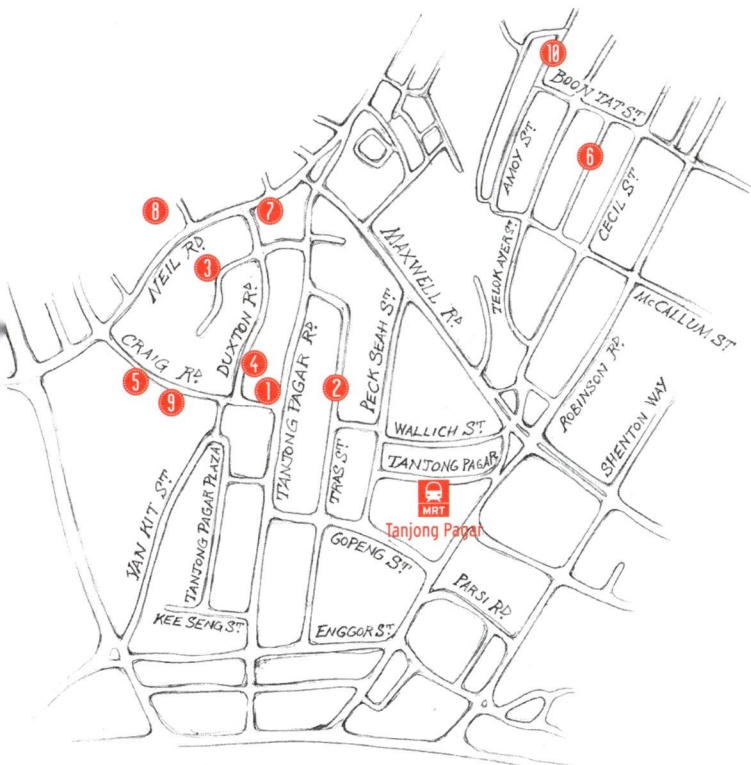

1 Blue Ginger
2 Brasserie Gavroche
3 Buyan
4 Culture Square
5 Fordham & Grand
6 Keystone Restaurant
7 Tea Chapter
8 The Gentleman's Press
9 Tong Mern Sern Antiques Arts & Crafts
10 Willow & Huxley

BLUE GINGER

Traditional Peranakan cuisine with a modern touch

97 Tanjong Pagar Road S(088518) / +65 6222 3928
thebluginger.com

Homemade food always brightens my day, be it cookies (thanks, mom), charred steak (thanks, dad), or satay babi and kuih pati (thanks Susan Teo, owner of Peranakan restaurant Blue Ginger). Peranakan cuisine (also called Nonya) is a unique blend of Chinese, Malay, and European influences, developed in the Straits Settlements in SE Asia. It is a must-try while you're in town. Although Nonya favorites can be a touchy subject with locals, this writer loves Blue Ginger. The traditional Peranakan dishes like beef rendang and sambal terong goreng are appropriately spiced for foreign taste buds so that you won't need gallons of water. When my own family visits, this is our first meal.

BRASSERIE GAVROCHE

Comforting French fare

66 Tras Street S(079005) / +65 6225 8266 / brasseriegavroche.com

You don't have to be a true-blue Francophile to appreciate this handsome establishment, brought to you courtesy of chef patron Frédéric Colin. A 1930s wooden bar counter rescued from the original Parisian Café de la Paix, black-and-white family photographs and mosaic floor tiles, all handpicked by his wife Charlotte, work together to channel a picture-perfect old school brasserie. The food, too, is a throwback to forgotten classics, with dishes like baked pork terrine pie with foie gras, and fish quenelles with an impossibly rich crayfish sauce made from recipes passed down from Colin's chef grandpa Henri. Excellent food, a respectable wine list and the charming ambiance make this a sure bet.

BUYAN

Haute Russian cuisine

9/10 Duxton Hill S(089593) / +65 6223 7008 / buyan.sg

I love blueberry blintzes, but beyond that most Russian meals I've tried left me cold. But Buyan has forced me to rethink. Their classic Russian dishes are masterfully executed and beautifully presented by young superstar Chef Kirill Shiryaev. Beluga caviar is delicately served on silver platters with pearl spoons and perfectly tender blinis. Aside from the food, Buyan has also amassed a rare wine collection worth more than $3.5 million. If you can't stretch to a bottle, many of the wines are available by the glass. Don't miss their wine museum featuring vintage tipples such as an 1841 Veuve Clicquot.

CULTURE SQUARE

Affordable Asian art

72 Duxton Road S(089531) / +65 6222 3283 / culture-square.com

Looking to spruce up those bare white walls? Culture Square is a great option for art aficionados (like me) who might not be in possession of bottomless pockets (also like me). They showcase affordable pieces by emerging artists from all over the world, my favorites being those depicting Asian scenery or dreamy cityscapes. I love gifting these to myself or as wedding presents or souvenirs for visitors. Each artwork is in a square format, all in varying sizes and priced under $1000. There are a ton of options to suit every taste or mood, from oils to collages, abstracts and watercolors.

FORDHAM & GRAND

Swanky late-night supper spot

43 Craig Road S(089681) / **+65 6221 3088** / fng.com.sg

I'm a bona fide night owl, which makes this joint – open till 3am – a real gem in my book. You have the handsome duo of Tron Young and Timothy Lim to thank for this cavernous speakeasy-styled bistro bar with an old world vibe, named after the notorious cross street in the Bronx back in the prohibition days. Well-executed classics like their value-for-money steak and fries never fail to satisfy, but it's their toothsome French toast with rum sabayon that makes me weak in the knees. Aside from stellar service, their mean cocktails and list of 100 wines under $100 round out this tidy package oh so nicely.

KEYSTONE RESTAURANT

Progressive European fine dining

11 Stanley Street S(068730) / +65 6221 0046
keystonerestaurant.com.sg

Growing up, my mom fed my siblings and I just about everything under the sun. Years later, I can safely say she has successfully cultivated in me what most would call an adventurous eater. As far as culinary risks go, this sophisticated setup care of restaurateur Eddie Han is a smart, calculated one. The well-heeled clientele come for both business lunches and romantic dinners showcasing seasonal ingredients plated up by chef Immanuel Tee, who cut his teeth at Guy Savoy. Give it a shot and you'll be pleased at how the molecular techniques used create unusual flavor and textural combinations to surprising effect.

TEA CHAPTER

All things tea

9 Neil Road S(088808) / +65 6226 1917 / tea-chapter.com.sg

Until moving to Asia, my knowledge of tea was largely limited to Lipton and hot toddies on a cold Boston evening. But after exploring some of the tea plantations in Vietnam and Sri Lanka, I have a newfound appreciation for the brewed leaf of the camellia sinensis plant. Tea Chapter is a hideaway tea paradise that sells handcrafted teapots and tea varieties for all tastes. They also offer tea art classes and a quiet second floor respite for peaceful conversation over your cuppa. Look out for photos of Great Britain's Queen Elizabeth, who famously dropped by in 1989. Quite the endorsement, don't you think?

THE GENTLEMEN'S PRESS

Stylish letterpress calendars and stationery

64 Neil Road S(088834) / +65 6222 6964
facebook.com/thegentlemenspress

I dabble in the art of antiquarian book restoration. Really, I do. So when I first walked into The Gentlemen's Press, my mouth dropped open in awe at the vintage letterpresses scattered throughout. The studio is the brainchild of Michelle Yu and Shian Ng, friends who met during art school and bonded over a mutual hankering for letterpress. Both their artistic styles mimic 19th century broadside colors and design, which they've worked into their hand-printed stationery, calendars, and business cards. In true letterpress style, they're happy to discuss custom projects and collaborations, so bring your ideas and let Michelle and Shian show you just how talented they are.

TONG MERN SERN ANTIQUES ARTS & CRAFTS

Hard-to-find Asian antiques

51 Craig Road S(089689) / **+65 6734 0761, +65 6223 1037**
tmsantiques.com

Karang guni men are collectors of other people's rubbish. They take it away, repair, polish, and sell it on to someone like Mr. Keng Ah Wong, who has curated Tong Mern Sern Antiques for more than 30 years. If restored Asian furniture, antique gold leafed buddha heads, and vintage music boxes are your thing, don't pass this shop by. Not that it's easily missed – there's a giant yellow banner above the front door reading, "We buy junk and sell antiques, some fools buy some fools sell." He may not have a tidy shop, but clearly Mr. Keng has a good sense of humor.

WILLOW & HUXLEY

Glam gal threads

20 Amoy Street S(069855) / +65 6220 1745 / willowandhuxley.com

Owners Laura Sisterson and Susie Wallace have brought together a clothing collection that makes Willow & Huxley the fashion equivalent of a candy store. There's natty tailoring, quirky prints, laidback boho-chic maxis and much more – Carrie Bradshaw, eat your heart out. The girls are fantastic stylists and if you're after something specific, be sure to pipe up as they can pull new arrivals or select vintage pieces from their secret stash if you ask nicely. Even my otherwise strong-willed gal pals turn into indecisive mush when they shop here and end up buying everything in sight. Don't say I didn't warn you.

ALKAFF BRIDGE
Robertson Quay

HELIX BRIDGE
next to Marina Bay Sands

HENDERSON WAVES BRIDGE
Southern Ridges trail

SKYBRIDGE OF THE PINNACLE@DUXTON
50th floor The Pinnacle@Duxton,
1 Cantonment Road S(080001)
pinnacleduxton.com.sg

bridges of singapore

Inspiring architectural works worth exploring

It's a good thing that urban architects have taken it upon themselves to ensure that our city's bridges are not only functional, but also unique artistic achievements. Of all the interesting bridges here (and there are many), I'd like to point you to four that epitomize creativity and ingenuity. The **Helix Bridge** resembles a steel strand of DNA and claims to be the world's first curved bridge, while **Henderson Waves Bridge** links two sections of our **Southern Ridges Trail** (see Green Spaces page 60) and is Singapore's highest pedestrian bridge. An often overlooked gem, the **skybridge of The Pinnacle@Duxton** offers a full 360 degree view of Singapore's waterfront, cityscape and historic shophouse district. Be clever and sneak a bottle of vino up – it's the best secret date spot in town. Finally, there's **Alkaff Bridge** near Robertson Quay – artist Pacita Abad used 55 different colors and more than 900 liters of paint to transform it into our most colorful bridge.

tiong bahru

I've got a bit of a soft spot for this once-sleepy, now hipster cool residential district. Though it's currently dominated by coffee joints, pretty boutiques, independent bookshops (see page 46) and cool eateries, elements of old like the conserved bird corner still exist. Perhaps it's the good-looking Art Deco architecture of the pre-war walkups with spiral staircases. Or maybe it's the fond memories I have of tagging along with my mom and grandma on their regular visits to Tiong Bahru Market. Then again, it might just have something to do with the many scrumptious food options available at one of the oldest housing estates in Singapore.

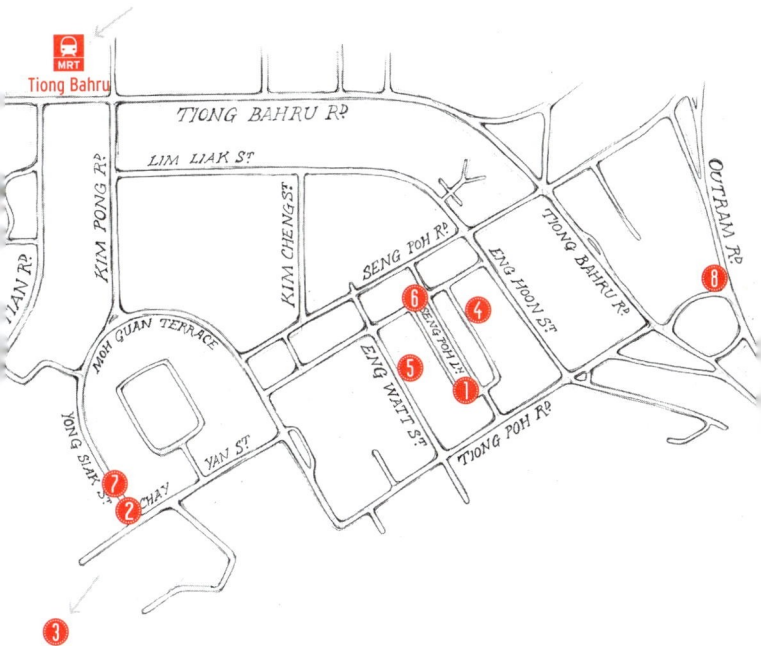

MRT
Tiong Bahru

TIONG BAHRU RD.

LIM LIAK ST.

KIM PONG RD.

KIM CHENG ST.

SENG POH RD.

SENG POH RD.

ENG HOON ST.

TIONG BAHRU RD.

OUTRAM RD.

MOH GUAN TERRACE

ENG WATT ST.

YONG SIAK ST.

CHAY

YAN ST.

TIONG POH RD.

LIAN RD.

1	Flea & Trees	5	Nimble/Knead
2	IKYU	6	Por Kee Eating House
3	Kevin Seah Bespoke (off map)	7	Strangelets
4	Nana & Bird	8	Tiong Bahru Pau

FLEA & TREES

Quirky collectables and women's clothing

#01-10, 68 Seng Poh Lane S(160068) / **+65 8139 1133**
facebook.com/fleatrees

For many years, Tiong Bahru was known as Mei Ren Wu ("den of beauties") because Singapore's rich men housed their mistresses here. I can only imagine what those same ladies would have made of the vintage collectables and other eclectic goodies that local designer Terence Yeung and his fashion consultant wife have curated at Flea & Trees. My favorite touch is an old chandelier that is now used as a plant hanger. Those seeking bright but tasteful jewelry or ye-olde-world fashion are sure to find something that pleases in this little den of beauty.

IKYU

Contemporary Japanese bites

5 Yong Siak Street S(168643) / +65 6223 9003 / ikyu.com.sg

IKYU isn't one of those typical dime a dozen Japanese restaurants — all pale wood and zen. Instead, this hip eatery's black metal furniture and gunmetal gray color palette give it a distinctly raw, urban feel. Taking the reins in the kitchen is the likable Takuma Seki, who dishes out items like Hokkaido scallop truffle carpaccio and robata (grilled) miso black cod, as well as sashimi and nigirizushi for the purists. Opt for an omakase set and try to score yourself the best seats in the house at the sushi counter, so you can sample their offerings while watching Seki-san and his chefs in action.

KEVIN SEAH BESPOKE

Bespoke menswear with old-world class

5 Jalan Kilang S(159405) / +65 9188 4681 / kevinseah.com.sg

If Singapore had such a thing as an official "style ambassador", the position would long since have been held by the local king of fashion, Kevin Seah. Although he's been featured in countless magazines, they always fail to mention just how gentlemanly he actually is. And we don't mean his garb. Yes, he's a style beacon. Yes, his bespoke line of menswear is Saville Row worthy. Yes, heads turn when he enters a room. But he's also one of the most affable, down to earth gentlemen that you'll ever meet. A fitting with Mr. Seah will put a spring in your step, a smile on your face and leave you feeling like fashion royalty.

NANA & BIRD

Stylish design collections

#01-65, 59 Eng Hoon Street S(160059) / **+65 9117 0430**
nanaandbird.com

Malls and their ubiquitous, Rihanna-blaring shops give me a headache.
I'd much rather shop in a standalone boutique that's designed their
environs with as much care and thought as they've given to the
selection of merchandise. This bird is one such place. Design doyens,
shopaholics and best friends Georgina Koh and Tan Chiew Ling bring
local and international labels for women to the Tiong Bahru 'hood.
You've got handmade ballet pumps by A Flat, gorgeous leather bags
by US-based Building Block, and flowy, feminine dresses by homegrown
brand Aijek. A place where I like to linger.

NIMBLE/KNEAD

Unconventional spa in a shipping container

#01-28, 66 Eng Watt Street S(160066) / +65 6438 3933
nimbleknead.com

Massages are one of my guilty pleasures. In my ideal world, I'd have a masseuse on call 24/7. In the meantime, I head to this nifty spot when I'm in need of a rubdown. The utilitarian space, (think bare concrete flooring and steel container walls), is a refreshing change from the usual spa interior design. They offer body masks and scrubs, as well as foot reflexology, but my treatment of choice is their signature Destination Bali, an Indonesian massage that uses long, soothing strokes and firm kneading to ease muscle aches and always leaves me feeling lighter and relaxed. Oh, and prices are easy on the wallet, too.

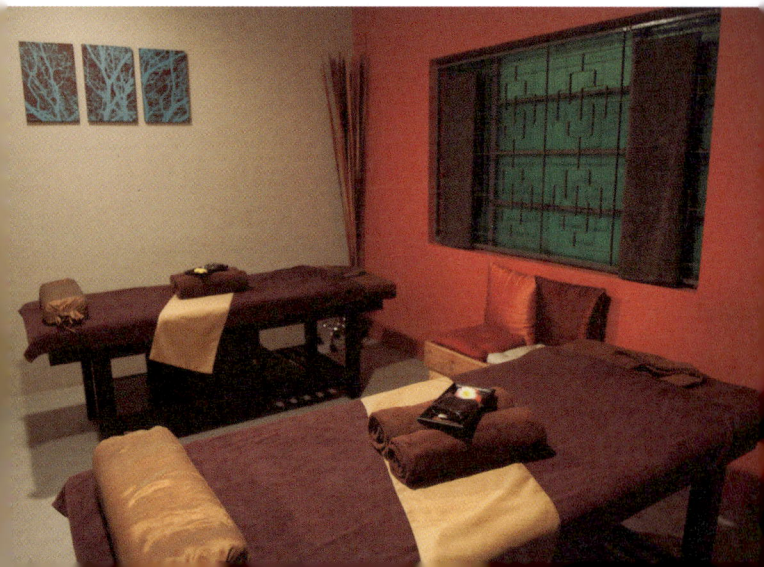

POR KEE EATING HOUSE

Scrumptious old school Chinese fare

#01-02, 69 Seng Poh Lane S(160069) / +65 6221 0582

I take all my favorite people to eat in a Tiong Bahru car park. That's right, nothing but the best! Though it may sound a little wonky, this *tze char* ("cook and fry") restaurant nestled among the heritage art deco flats of Singapore's hippest 'hood serves up fresh live seafood and wallet-friendly home-style Chinese dishes. The sticky black Champagne pork ribs are delicious, the house fried rice is perfection, and Por Kee has a reputation for serving Singapore's best sweet and sour anything. If you want to fit right in like a regular, order the silken homemade tofu braised with mushrooms.

STRANGELETS
Artfully designed objects

7 Yong Siak Street S(168644) / +65 6222 1456 / strangelets.sg

In this quirky little shop, you'll find a smattering of artfully designed objects from around the globe. Four partners (of mixed heritages, but all with a background in architecture or design) set out to create a unique space to showcase what they call "militant craftsmanship" – or the quality of uniqueness. The foursome trawl the ends of the earth to collect handcrafted whimsical objects from chic designers like Geoffrey Mance and Astier de Villatte – think wooden (working) radios and tomato soaps. There are even blood red chandeliers (inspired by hedgehog bristles) for those looking to invest in a little something different.

TIONG BAHRU PAU

Best buns in Singapore

#02-09, 237 Outram Road S(169041) / +65 6222 7656

The streets of Singapore were once packed with food vendors. But in the 1960s, in an attempt to clean up the streets, the government offered free space to those vendors willing to relocate to permanent collective food centers. Voila! The famous hawker centers were born! Tiong Bahru Pau began in just this way and has been family-run and famous ever since. Nowadays you can find pau (steamed buns with a variety of fillings) everywhere from 7-11s to airlines, but if you're craving the best airy, tender buns in town, head to TBP. Their char siew (BBQ pork) buns have an outer skin that melts so quickly in the mouth, it melts your heart.

indie bookstores

Top spots to pick up a good read

BOOKS ACTUALLY
9 Yong Siak Street S(168645) +65 6222 9195
booksactually.com

LITTERED WITH BOOKS
20 Duxton Road S(089486) +65 6220 6824
litteredwithbooks.com

WOODS IN THE BOOKS
3 Yong Siak Street S(168642) +65 6222 9980
woodsinthebooks.sg

BOOKS ACTUALLY

My absolute favorite place to spend an afternoon is at a good bookstore. At the top of my list is **Books Actually**. Owner Kenny Leck stocks the widest range of Singaporean titles in town and fills his backroom with vintage tchotchkes from around the region. In addition, he somehow finds time to champion local writers by publishing them under his Math Paper Press, Indie gem **Littered With Books**, shared in a two-storey shophouse, overflowing with a multitude of different literary genres. Grab a chair by the window and read the day away. For children's books, pop by **Woods in the Books**, a fabulous spot run by Shannon Ong and illustrator Mike Foo. Mike is usually busy drawing, but he's happy to offer suggestions or guide you through his own illustrated works.

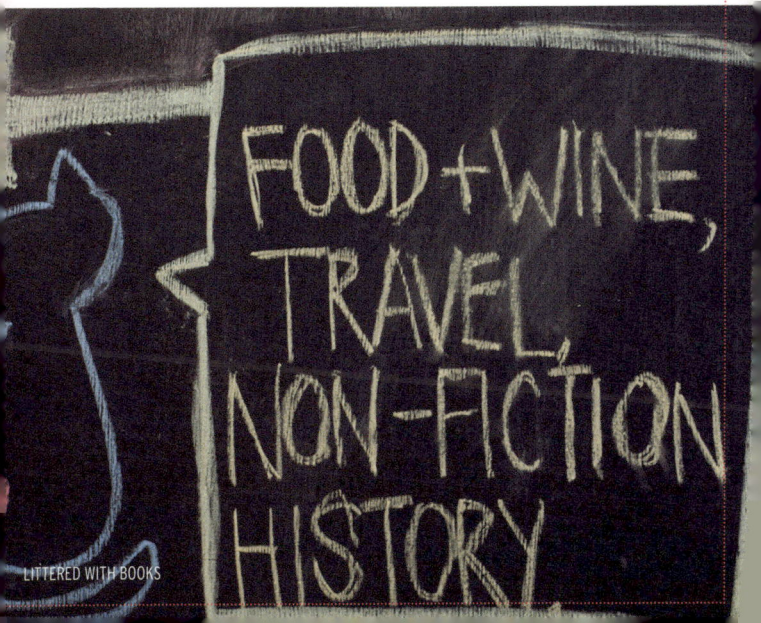

LITTERED WITH BOOKS

bukit timah

dempsey hill, holland village

Singapore's known as the garden city, and there's no better place to get a dose of nature than out by residential neighborhood Bukit Timah, centered around the well-manicured Singapore Botanic Gardens, home to the world's most extensive collection of tropical orchids (including our national flower). There's more greenery to be had at Bukit Timah Nature Reserve, where you'll find Bukit Timah Hill, the tallest peak in Singapore. Also worth a visit are lifestyle destinations like Holland Village, (now more easily accessible thanks to the MRT circle line) and woodsy Dempsey Hill (take a cab to this former colonial British army barracks).

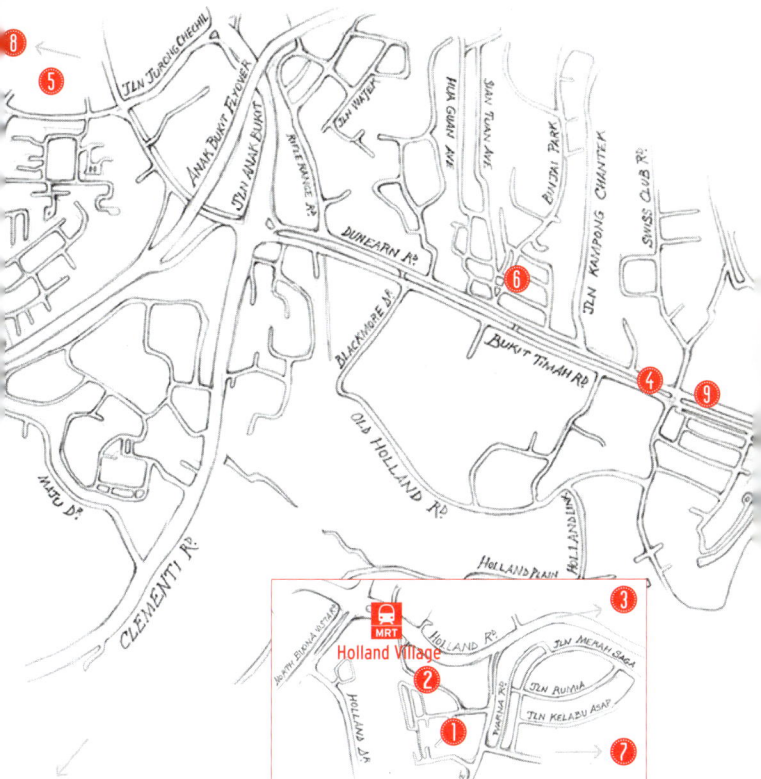

Map labels:

JLN JURONG CHECHU
JLN WAJEK
HUA GUAN AVE
SIAN TUAN AVE
BINJAI PARK
JLN KAMPONG CHANTEK
SWISS CLUB RD
ANAK BUKIT FLYOVER
JLN ANAK BUKIT
RIFLE RANGE RD
DUNEARN RD
BLACKMORE DR
OLD HOLLAND RD
BUKIT TIMAH RD
MATU DR
CLEMENTI RD
HOLLAND PLAIN
HOLLAND LINK
HOLLAND RD
NORTH BUONA VISTA
HOLLAND DR
TAMAN WARNA
JLN MERAH SAGA
JLN RUMIA
JLN KELABU ASAP
HOLLAND AVE

MRT Holland Village

MRT Clementi

HOLLAND VILLAGE

1	2am:dessertbar	6	Hanna Lee
2	Antipodean	7	Little Man
3	Au Jardin	8	The Disgruntled Chef
4	Blu Kouzina	9	Thow Kwang Pottery Jungle (off map)
5	Carpenter & Cook	10	Violet Oon's Kitchen

49

2AM:DESSERTBAR

Best desserts in Singapore

21a Lorong Liput S(277733) / +65 6291 9727 / 2amdessertbar.com

Ask me about 2am:dessertbar and my legs go wobbly. I trail off mid-sentence, flail for the right words, and my eyes go misty. I mean where else in this town can one find basil white chocolate, black pepper, passion fruit, and Japanese sea grapes all in one edible, magically plated work of art? Chef Janice Wong's experimental creations are downright spectacular. Since 2am is designed to be a late-night lounge, the lights are low, couches plush, and the wine list carefully curated. This should be the first place you think of when your date says, "So, now where to?"

ANTIPODEAN

Flirty women's clothing and homewares

27a Lorong Mambong S(277686) / +65 6463 7336
antipodeanshop.com

From stargazing in the desert outback to relaxing on Sydney's beaches or taking in the sophisticated charm of Melbourne's bistros—there's always excitement in Australia. Cynthia Liang, who spent many years living down under, has brought back to our shores a taste of this excitement. The bright second floor space just off the main drag of Holland Village showcases the work of some of Cynthia's favorite Australian designers. You'll find colorful sundresses, zebra striped platforms, and vintage sunnies nesting with sexy burgundy eveningwear. Don't hesitate to show off your new look just downstairs at any one of the many bustling al fresco restaurants and bars.

AU JARDIN

Classic French cuisine

EJH Corner House, Singapore Botanic Garden Visitors Centre, Cluny Road S(259569) / +65 6466-8812 / lesamis.com.sg

This fancy French restaurant in a colonial black and white house uses the lush Botanic Garden setting to full advantage. If you are looking for an evening of romance and sophistication, this is the spot. A stellar wine list complements the classic cuisine, and the service is flawless. If you'd rather dine al fresco to fully take in the surroundings, request a table on the terrace when you book. If the relationship with your travelling buddy is of a more platonic nature, I'd suggest a splash-out lunch or prix-fixe Sunday brunch following a morning visit to the famous National Orchid Garden.

BLU KOUZINA

Homestyle Greek fare

893 Bukit Timah Road S(589615) / +65 6875 0872 / blukouzina.com

Last time I visited Athens, the train was out of service and I had to bribe my way into town by offering to buy the cabbie a beer. After some haggling and a rather harrowing ride, he joined me at a cafe within sight of the Acropolis where we dined on creamy cheeses, salty dips with fresh pita and ouzo... oh the ouzo! Since then I've hunted for a neighborhood Greek bistro that lives up to that memory. By all the wisdom of the ancients, it shouldn't be hiding in Singapore – but here it is. If I close my eyes, breathe in deeply and tip back ouzo at Blu Kouzina, I'm back laughing with that cabbie.

CARPENTER & COOK

Sweet treats in a vintage-styled café

#01-06, 19 Lorong Kilat S(598120) / +65 6463 3648
carpenterandcook.com

If you've got two passions in life, why not combine them? That's what the folks behind this cozy café did. Carpenter Phoebe outfitted the venue with quirky vintage wooden tables and chairs, and a collection of charming antiques. But what keeps me coming back are the delish homemade goodies like raspberry peach mini bundts, passion fruit meringue tarts and sticky toffee brownies, courtesy of Le Cordon Bleu-trained chef and co-owner Shenn Sim, the cook of the duo. They also make their own jams in flavors such as pear and fig. I can't say no to their chocolate sea salt caramel tart either (yes, it's as luscious as it sounds).

HANNA LEE

Queen of bling

#02-15 Cluny Court
501 Bukit Timah Road S(259760)
+65 6463 2698 / shophannalee.com

Looking for fabulous arm swag,
statement necklaces, or ear candy?
Look no further than Hanna Lee. Her
pieces are fun, glam and come in a
variety of colors and materials that
are ideal for mixing and matching.
You've got drop earrings in semi-
precious stones like labradorite;
rose gold bracelets, and delicate
chain necklaces for layering and
draping. Plus, there's more playful
stuff in enamel, cute beads, bright
neon threads and leathers. Bold
baubles aplenty make for a magpie
heaven. You'll be cooing and oohing
over all the prettiness as soon as you
enter. Yes, even you, hardened shopper.

LITTLE MAN

Hip boutique in the suburbs

7c Binjai Park S(589821) / +65 6464 6515 / shoplittleman.com

Tucked away in the suburban landscape of Binjai Park is a hipster haven chock-full of natty bow ties, ironic iPhone covers, graphic tees, traveler's notebooks, indie fashion labels for men and women including in-house label AL&ALICIA, and contemporary furniture. Little Man is an imaginary character dreamed up by the shop's owners, architect Ian and designer Alicia. The wee gentleman may be of diminutive stature, but he makes up for it with oodles of style and taste. It's an, ahem, tall order to fill an entire shop where each and every piece is utterly droolworthy, but Ian and Alicia do. It's kooky, it's cool and there's something for everyone.

THE DISGRUNTLED CHEF

Modern European communal dining

26b Dempsey Road S(247693) / +65 6476 5305 / disgruntledchef.com

It's all about sharing at chef and owner Daniel Sia's Dempsey Hill stalwart. While I'm not usually a fan of the small plates concept (which is often just an excuse for serving tiny plates with huge prices), this industrial chic eatery does one hell of a job. I've been known to fight my better half for highlights such as the moreish baked bone marrow with braised oxtail, steak tartare accompanied by truffle hash browns, and chili-cumin lamb short ribs. There are also some mean drinks to be had like The Dempsey Belle, a unique vodka-based tipple with raspberries, rosemary, red pepper and lime.

THOW KWANG POTTERY JUNGLE

Pottery and porcelain beyond your wildest imagination

85 Lorong Tawas S(639823) / **+65 6268 6121**
facebook.com/tkpotteryjungle

Discovering the gem that is Thow Kwang took me back to boyhood days. To when my father used to take me to discover hidden treasures in the antique shops nestled in the backwood hills of Arkansas. Not only does family-run Thow Kwang have one of the last remaining "dragon kilns" in Singapore, it's packed with Asian ceramics of all kinds. It's easy to forget you're in Singapore while weaving through their dusty corridors. Shelving reaches up higher than you can reach and there are plenty of hidden attics filled with masterworks if you can convince the staff to lead you there.

VIOLET OON'S KITCHEN

Singapore's doyenne of dining

881 Bukit Timah Road S(279893) / +65 6468 5430
violetoonskitchen.com

This Peranakan "first lady of food" learned her cooking skills from nonya aunties and started her career as a food columnist. Madam Oon's breezy Bukit Timah restaurant references the black and white bungalows of her youth and is overseen by her son Ming. The menu offers a blend of Peranakan classics, comfort food (like ViO's Shepherd's Pie) and fusion favorites perfected over the last 30 years. Try her dry laksa — all the flavors of this classic dish are concentrated into a sauce and served pasta-style — and kueh bengka, a dense, subtly sweet tapioca cake served with coconut cream and gula melaka syrup.

green spaces for nature lovers

The great outdoors

I've hosted many visitors to Singapore over the years, taking them through the skyscraper-dominated landscape of our fine garden city. However, when nature lovers visit, I make sure to bring them to the **Kranji Countryside**, a perfect rural spot to spend an afternoon. Tucked away down winding lanes are charming locally-owned farms like Hay Dairies and Jurong Frog Farm, that sell everything from fruit and veggies to frogs and koi fish. If what you're after is a tranquil trek, then try the **Southern Ridges Trail**. The trail stretches nine kilometers through and over lush hills, past manicured gardens, all the while offering a panorama of Singapore's skyline. Go in the morning before it gets too hot or in the cool of early evening. Watch out for monkeys swinging in the trees – it should go without saying, but just in case, don't feed those cheeky buggers. For those of you looking to get a sense of what life in Singapore used to be like back in the '60s, there's **Pulau Ubin**. This rustic island just off Singapore's northeastern coast is famous for its fresh seafood, cheerful villagers and relaxing jungle biking trails. To reach Ubin, you'll need to hop on an inexpensive ferry (likely captained by a gruff old grandpa) from Changi Jetty. On the trip over keep an eye out for the kelongs (floating fishing villages). While you're biking around, don't miss Chek Jawa, a wetland reserve with a pristine shoreline.

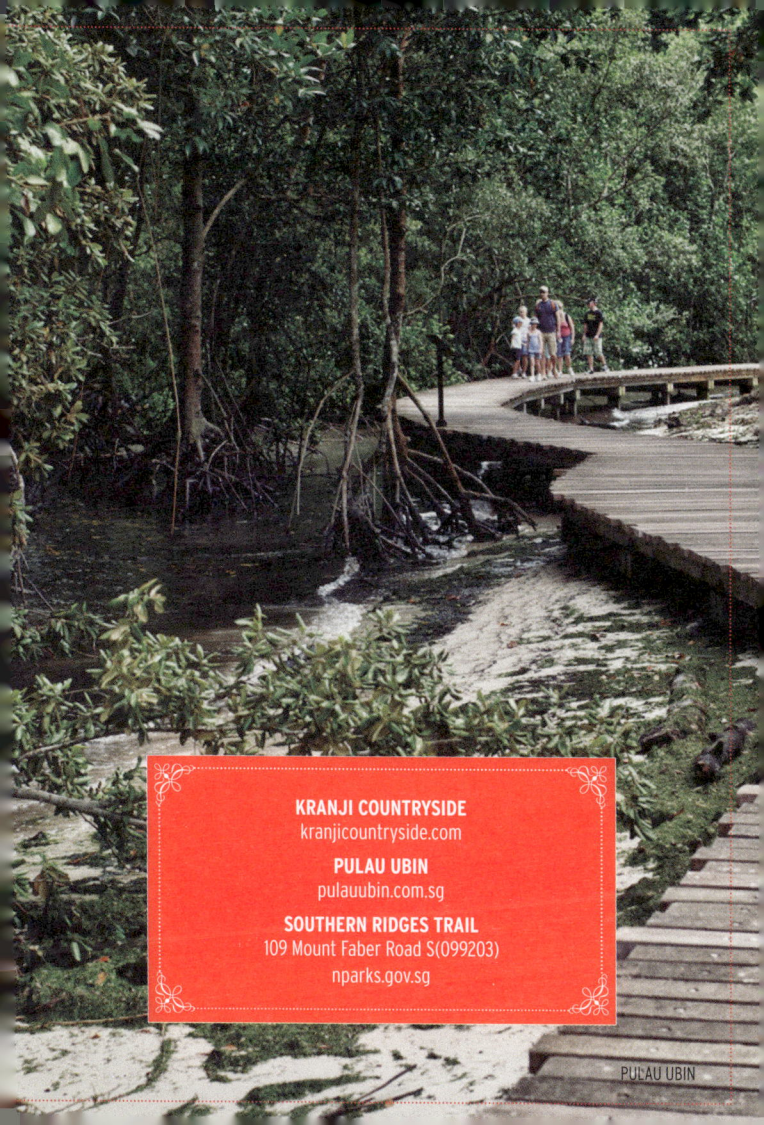

KRANJI COUNTRYSIDE
kranjicountryside.com

PULAU UBIN
pulauubin.com.sg

SOUTHERN RIDGES TRAIL
109 Mount Faber Road S(099203)
nparks.gov.sg

PULAU UBIN

orchard

Orchard Road is Singapore's shrine to the gods of consumerism. One of the great retail centers of the world, the entire strip is lined with shiny, air-conditioned malls – a great refuge from the heat, regardless of how you feel about shopping centers. Quite a change really from the various fruit and spice orchards that used to dominate it back in the day (hence the name.) The sheer array of high street brands, luxe labels and independent multi-label boutiques – featuring both Asian and international designers – is impressive enough to lure even a crowd-averse individual like myself. No mean feat let me tell you.

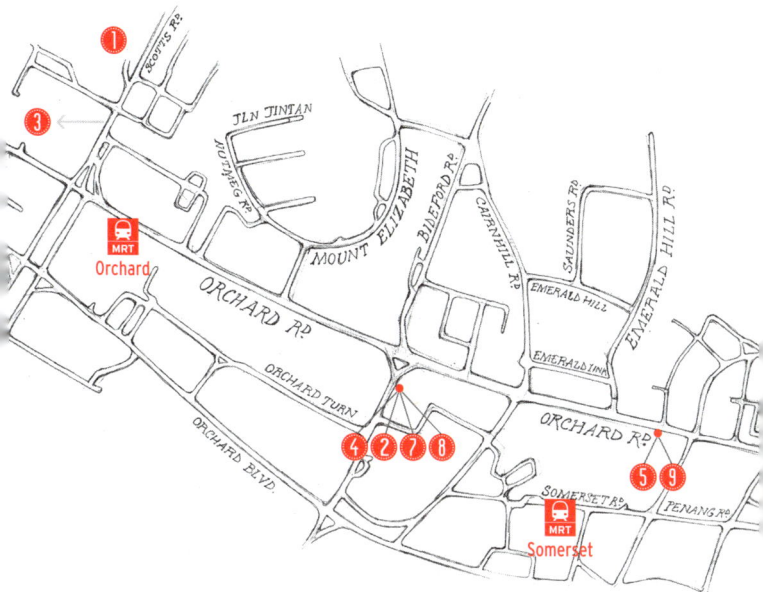

1 &MADE
2 Ambush
3 Antoinette (off map)
4 Atomi
5 Blackmarket no. 2

6 Fred Lives Here
7 Hansel
8 Inhabit
9 PACT

Map labels: SCOTTS RD, JLN JINTAN, NUTMEG RD, BIDEFORD RD, MOUNT ELIZABETH, CAIRNHILL RD, SAUNDERS RD, EMERALD HILL, EMERALD HILL RD, EMERALD LINK, MRT Orchard, ORCHARD RD, ORCHARD TURN, ORCHARD BLVD, ORCHARD RD, SOMERSET RD, PENANG RD, MRT Somerset

&MADE

Stellar gourmet burgers

#01-04/05/06 Pacific Plaza, 9 Scotts Road S(228210)
+65 6732 9808 / andmade.sg

Celeb chef Bruno Ménard's casual yet quirky diner serves up comfort grub at approachable prices. From the old school eight-bit Space Invaders design motifs (the handiwork of local design firm Stripe Collective) to the menu of milkshakes and fries, the place is custom made for the kid in all of us. Order the popular dry-aged beef 'B' Burger and The 3 Little Pigs, made with bacon, chorizo and pork belly, dressed with yuzu kosho (pepper) mayo and roasted sesame sauce. I have yet to find a better burger joint in this city. Plus, it also houses L'Entrecote Express, its steak frites sister restaurant. Score.

AMBUSH

Edgy menswear

#03-14 Mandarin Gallery, 333a Orchard Road S(238897)
+65 6836 7667 / ambushstore.com

Though it may have a ways to go, Singapore is without a doubt becoming edgier. Personally, I'm loving it. Creative graffiti (albeit officially authorized, so hold that spray gun) and serious skating is showing up, and it's not uncommon to find hipster bike crews zipping around town on custom fixies wearing hoodies and flipped back messenger hats. Ambush is clearly going after this urban hipster crowd – young and sexy with a t-shirt fetish. Skull & crossbone cufflinks are complemented nicely by crushed leather jackets and camo shorts. You still can't buy gum here, but jaywalking in your glam-punk studded boots is unlikely to get you in trouble.

ANTOINETTE

French-inspired pâtisserie and tea salon

#B1-08/09/10 Palais Renaissance, 390 Orchard Road S(238871)
+65 6735 6392 / antoinette.com.sg

When it comes to sweets, few things get me quite as excited as macarons. I've been known to bring boxes of Pierre Hermé's back from Paris. Few places in Singapore make as mean a version as local pâtisserie Antoinette, helmed by celebrated pastry chef Pang Kok Keong. The Brittany — caramel spiked with fleur de sel (sea salt) — is exceptional, particularly when accompanied by hot tea such as osmanthus sencha or their signature Earl Grey d'antoinette. There are over 20 different custom-blended teas and infusions to choose from, and their range of sweet and savory crêpes is no slouch either. The brilliant Nutella-filled Nougatine is a personal favorite of mine.

ATOMI

Handcrafted Japanese homeware and accessories

#04-27 Mandarin Gallery, 333a Orchard Road S(238897)
+65 6887 4138 / atomi-jp.com

The Japanese make outstanding products. Unfortunately, the most artistic products are handmade by master craftsmen living in remote areas that are generally a challenge to reach. That's where Atomi comes in. Owner Mitsuko Murano travels to the far reaches of her native homeland in search of these artisans, bringing back the spoils of her adventures . She's collected everything from Naoto Fukasawa's organically shaped wooden chairs to Shotoku Glass Company's light bulb-thin usuhari glassware. If handcrafted homewares are on your shopping list, Atomi is a must-visit.

BLACKMARKET NO. 2

Fashion-forward clothing and accessories

#02-10 Orchard Central, 181 Orchard Road S(238896)
+65 6634 5201 / theblackmarket.sg

Ever since taking this job, I've wanted to change my look. I want
to be a bit – dare I say, hipper. I could of course just check-out The
Sartorialist blog and grab a credit card. But I'd like my makeover
to be a little more subtle, a little more paced. And that's why I love
Blackmarket. While the clothes here are edgy enough to turn a few
heads, I'm comfortable walking down the street and integrating
pieces into my current wardrobe. I don't know when I'll take that next
leap of fashiondom faith, but when I do – watch out world.

FRED LIVES HERE

Funky one-of-a-kind décor

108 Emerald Hill Road S(229385) / **+65 9641 7727** / fredliveshere.com

Ex-makeup artist Angie Pasley has an eye for beauty, and not necessarily the conventional kind. She takes modern classics from the likes of Eames, Wegner, Jacobsen et al and reinvents them into something quite remarkable. There are also antiques, custom-made bits and retro wares galore in her shophouse. Truthfully, it feels like stepping into Alice's wonderland — everything is just a little bit surprising. Artworks masquerade as trays. Mirrors come perched on duck feet. That Eames lounge chair, upon closer inspection, it's made of concrete. Yes, concrete. Possibly the coolest piece of outdoor furniture ever, from what's definitely one of the coolest showrooms ever.

HANSEL

Whimsical, flirty womenswear

#02-14 Mandarin Gallery, 333a Orchard Road S(238897)
+65 6836 5367 / ilovehansel.com

Like our little island, homegrown brand Hansel is pretty damn hot these days. It's the local fashion label of bespectacled designer Jo Soh, who's been making big waves in Asia's fashion scene for the last few years. Her flirty print jumpsuits are paired with whimsical dresses, wraps, and blouses. Yes, I'm a guy, but I do know a thing or two about accessories. So does Ms Soh, who also includes unique playful jewelry like a red and gold watermelon brooch or hand-carved wooden donkey necklace in her collection. Soh's line is versatile and can be worn day or night. Fashionistas, get your groove on.

INHABIT

Progressive fashion for men and women

#02-16 Mandarin Gallery, 333a Orchard Road S(238897)
+65 6836 8441 / inhabit.com.sg

I adore hats. As such, you can understand why I fell for Inhabit the moment I saw their hats in the front window. Beyond beautiful millinery, this boutique offers high-end women's wear curated from fashion houses around the world. They also showcase a lovely selection of lesser-known Singaporean jewelry artists, whose bangles make excellent gifts for your loved ones back home. Then again, a hat makes an excellent gift as well (hint hint).

PACT

Trendy retailer/eaterie/barber

#02-16/19 Orchard Central, 181 Orchard Road S(238896)
+65 6884 4143 / visitpact.com

You've got to do something a little different in retail-heavy Orchard Road to stand out. Three-in-one concept store PACT does exactly that. This minimalist high-ceilinged, collaborative effort houses restaurant/bar Kilo's cuisine (see page 97), Japanese hair salon +LIM and multi-label fashion boutique K.I.N (Know It Nothing). Clued-in shoppers will want to head straight to clothing and accessories store K.I.N which stocks goods such as Imperial Barber Products, shades, functional Fabrix tote bags and tees from local brand Nom Nom, starring street food specialties including nasi lemak and ice kachang.

coffee specialists

Give me that caffeine

40 HANDS
#01-12 Block 78 Yong Siak Street S(163078) +65 6225 8545
40handscoffee.com

CHYE SENG HUAT HARDWARE
150 Tyrwhitt Road, S(207563) +65 6396 0609
cshhcoffee.com

NYLON COFFEE ROASTERS
#01-40, 4 Everton Park S(080004) +65 6220 2330
nyloncoffee.sg

ORIOLE COFFEE ROASTERS
10/10a Jiak Chuan Road S(089264) +65 6224 8131
oriolecoffee.com

I've tried to quit coffee a few times, but I'm past all that now – I freely admit that I'm addicted to the stuff. One of the first things I look for when I go someplace new is a locally-owned café. They're a great place to strike up conversation and get to know new people and locales. Here are my faves: **Oriole Coffee Roasters** for heritage charm and gourmet brews, **Chye Seng Huat Hardware** (see page 109) for the quirkiness of it, **Nylon Coffee Roasters** for their dedication to the third wave coffee movement and **40 Hands** for their sustainable roasts (guess how many hands a bean passes through from tree to mug).

central

bugis

The central business district (or CBD for short) – Singaporeans have a real penchant for acronyms – stretches from the shiny high-rises of Raffles Place to Marina Bay to City Hall to form the ever-iconic gleaming skyline of Singapore. For the worker ants (myself included), there's a wealth of cafés, bars and restaurants (business lunch deals are king in the area) peppered around the city's colonial, cultural and religious sites including performing arts venue Esplanade (aka the "durian" by locals), the Asian Civilisations Museum and two statues of Sir Stamford Raffles (in black and white – have fun locating both).

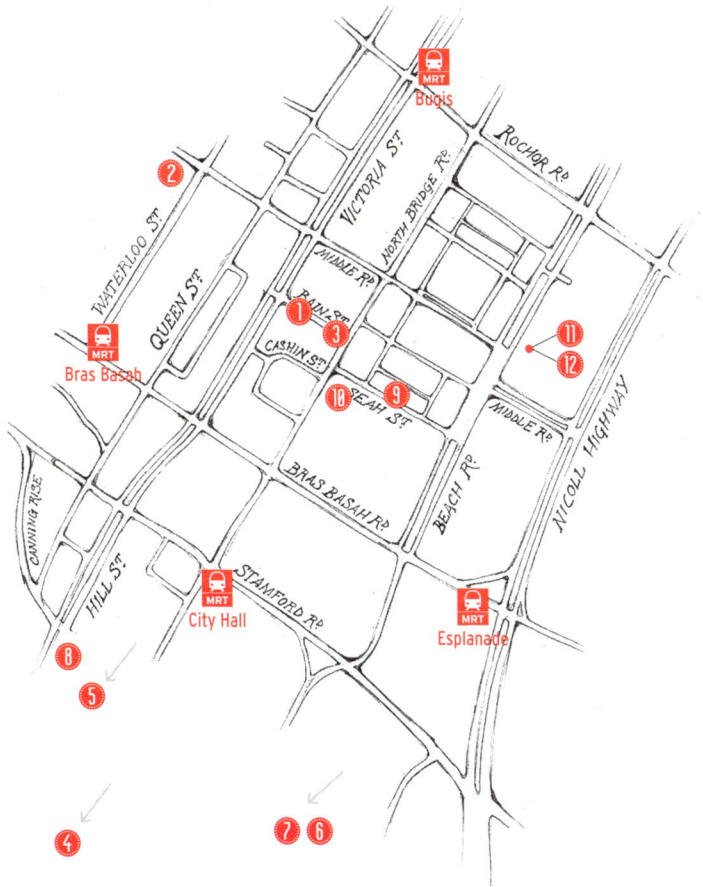

1   Art Gallery 3
2   Artichoke
3   Cat Socrates
4   Fiftyfive (off map)
5   Granny's Day Out (off map)
6   Olivia Cassivelaun Fancourt (off map)

7   Ong Shunmugam (off map)
8   Roxy Disc House
9   Supermama
10   Surrender
11   Tom's Palette
12   Tong Tong Friendship Store

ART GALLERY 3

Tibetan Dzi beads and Chinese art

231 Bain street #02-89, Bras Basah Complex S(180231) /
+65 6333 4283

Indiana Jones was my childhood idol. I would park a brown fedora on my head and parade around humming his theme song for hours on end. When I want to rekindle that boyhood feeling I head to Art Gallery 3. Hidden away on the second floor of the Bras Basah Complex, the gallery is home to an interesting assortment of old Chinese statuaries, snuff bottles and burial trinkets. You will also find ancient Tibetan dzi beads (considered mystical in the Tibetan culture). Keep an eye out for the elderly gentleman selling artwork – he has the happiest face in all of Singapore.

ARTICHOKE

Modern Moorish cuisine

161 Middle Road S(188978) / **+65 6336 6949** / **artichoke.com.sg**

Behind a rustic orange one-room church is one of my favorite restaurants in the city and one I've recommended to countless people. Chef Bjorn Shen lovingly calls his Turkish-inspired cuisine "food with balls." I call it some of the most flavorful and interesting fare I've ever had in Singapore — or anywhere else for that matter. The moment you walk through the door, you're struck with the tantalizing aromas of roasting lamb and Moorish spices. Bjorn's manager Ronnie is always on hand to help you navigate through the exquisite sharing menu. Bring a big group and set aside the entire evening for a moreish Moorish immersion.

CAT SOCRATES

Whimsical gifts and toys

#02-25 Bras Basah Complex, 231 Bain Street S(180231)
+65 6333 0870 / catsocrates.com

It's not that I'm a quiet person. Really, I'm not. Yet sometimes even I need a quiet nook and Cat Socrates provides a delightful hideaway. You'll find this little bohemian shop on the second floor of the Bras Basah Complex, in an area better known for used school books and Chinese charms. In between whimsical tin robots and handmade journals, you'll also find vintage polka dot sundresses. If you're short on books, don't worry – Cat Socrates has plenty of titles to browse through. Or better yet, write a letter home on handmade stationery that the owners have collected on their journeys around Asia.

FIFTYFIVE

A boutique for the urbane gentleman

3rd Floor, 55b Boat Quay S(049844) / +65 9853 5378
facebook.com/fiftyfivesg

A partnership between the proprietors of Tyrwhitt General Company
(see page 114), Kevin Seah Bespoke (see page 40) and Ed Et Al is tucked
away in a shophouse along Boat Quay, this joint venture fashioned for
the sartorially-minded man carries an array of products from both local
and international talent alike. Handsome products such as frames from
Masunaga Eyewear (Japan) and bags from Brit label The Cambridge
Satchel Company cozy up beside homegrown wares, like K by Kevin
Seah's approachable yet stylish ready-to-wear and Ed Et Al's impeccable
handmade leather shoes. Brogues on, fellas.

GRANNY'S DAY OUT

Stylish vintage women's clothing

#03-25 Peninsula Shopping Centre, 3 Coleman Street S(179804)
+65 6336 9774 / grannysdayout.net

Vintage European and American fashion is all the rage these days in Singapore. While some well-kept tai tais have the time to shop the markets of Paris, thankfully there's Granny's Day Out for the rest. The swanky ladies at Granny's have traveled the globe collecting stylish women's wear from the 1930s to '80s to help you jump start your chic factor. Be a star in a playful 70s bright yellow jumpsuit and silk headscarf, or go for the cowgirl look with feather-lined knee high boots and denim jacket. There's also a wide range of accessories such as vintage clutches and belts to complete your look.

OLIVIA CASSIVELAUN FANCOURT

Superb French nosh in a gorgeous setting

#02-02 The Arts House, 1 Old Parliament Lane S(179429)
+65 6333 9312 / ocf-singapore.com

Olivia Cassivelaun Fancourt (OCF) sure is a mouthful. But just so you know, this stunning restaurant housed in a conservation building along the water actually named after Sir Stamford Raffles' first wife (fitting really, as OCF overlooks Raffles' statue which marks his landing site along the Singapore River). Helmed by local chef Jonathan Koh, you can expect a season-driven menu of pretty French dishes served up in an elegant, tastefully done up space of gray, white and black. It's an undeniably romantic spot at night, though if you're with the boys there is a handsome balcony for cigars and whiskey.

ONG SHUNMUGAM

Contemporary cheongsam atelier

#B1-36 Hong Leong Building, 16 Raffles Quay S(048581)
+65 6223 4804 / ongshunmugam.com

Designer Priscilla Shunmugam, the brains (and beauty) behind the brand is mostly known for her reinterpretation of the classic cheongsam, incorporating beautiful traditional Southeast Asian textiles like batik mixed with geometric prints and lace in modern silhouettes like peplum waists and fierce shoulders. If you're looking for a showstopping cocktail dress, you've come to the right place. Alternatively, if you'd like to invoke your inner Charlie's Angel, opt for the Archway olive green jumpsuit, slap on the lippie, slick back your hair and you'll be ready to strut your way through the bars of Singapore.

ROXY DISC HOUSE

Vinyl audiophile heaven

#03-42 The Adephi, 1 Coleman Street S(179803) / +65 6336 6192

Do you remember the first album you owned? Mine was Richie Valens – I was 10 and I thought it was the coolest gift I'd ever been given. I remember playing La Bamba so often that my Dad nearly broke the tape. Music is a massive part of my life still, though these days I tend towards blues and folk with a side of ghetto groove. When the itch to browse consumes me, I head to Roxy. For nearly 50 years, music and vinyl lovers have considered it a second home, a place to discover forgotten gems and congregate as an audiophile community.

SUPERMAMA

Simple, beautiful objects

30a Seah Street S(188386) / +65 6338 3877 / supermama.sg

I'm forever thinking about how to unclutter my life. People tell me I'm organized, but I'm still trying to cut out the unnecessary and focus on buying only unfussy, timeless, well-crafted, USEFUL objects. Supermama is the first stop on this quest. Owner Edwin Low's curated boutique sells one-off exquisite objects crafted from organic, simple materials. Many of the items originate in Japan, like Tajika hand-forged shears and Futagami bottle openers. The thing that unites all the items sold here is their pure beauty. Low has an eye for the unique that is earning him praise around town.

SURRENDER

Sharp menswear

#02-31 Raffles Hotel Arcade, 328 North Bridge Road S(188719)
+65 6733 2130 / surrenderous.com

Surrender could easily be mistaken for just another lush men's store hyping up overpriced heritage brands to the fashion forward. But they're not. It's serious about helping clients discover classic style through unique brands. Old world charm abounds - Cire Trudon candles (since 1643), Saint-James sweaters (since 1889), and Moscot eyewear (since 1915) are all on offer. Put your faith in Danny and the rest of the team here. They have detailed knowledge of their brands and are eager to teach. After loading up, head downstairs to Raffles' famed billiard room for Cuban cigars and fine tipples. You'll need that new classy collar to meet the dress code.

TOM'S PALETTE

Homemade ice cream with local flavors

#01-25 Shaw Leisure Gallery, 100 Beach Road S(189702)
+65 6296 5239 / tomspalette.com.sg

Singapore is damn hot - make no mistake. There's only one place to cool off here: the movie theater, where, word of warning, it's so cold you'll almost certainly need a jacket. If you're not in the mood for that, head to Tom's Palette for some homemade ice cream. Tom's is a hidden gem but worth the effort needed to find it. Although they make traditional flavors like coffee and berry, they also have a plethora of uniquely Singaporean flavors such as the to-die-for salted egg yolk, lychee, and horlicks. Now that we've got a handle on cooling off, can we please do something about those frigid movie theaters?

TONG TONG FRIENDSHIP STORE

Sartorial Sino-chic

#01-04/05 Shaw Towers, 100 Beach Road S(189702)
+65 6396 3887 / tongtong.sg

Chinoiserie lovers, step into Tong Tong, a celebration of Sheau Yun's obsession with Chinese design and cultural history. So what is a 'Friendship Store' exactly? Back in 50's China, state-owned stores popped up to sell imported Western goods to foreigners. Funnily enough, they weren't particular friendly. Not like Tong Tong. The experience begins before you even set foot inside. A whimsical tiled tunnel welcomes you to the tree-fronted entrance, after which you'll find mandarin collar jackets in cheery colors, cheongsams in zany prints and a variety of whimsical accessories in this darling little store that imparts a tasteful hark back to days of yore.

SINGAPORE AFTER DARK:
top-notch cocktail bars in town

Sip on some delish tipples at these watering holes

Thanks to an increasingly sophisticated local cocktail culture, there's no shortage of drinking spots in Singapore. Haji Lane stalwart **Bar Stories** in Kampong Glam (see page 92) is one of the pioneers of the bespoke cocktail trend in town, you'll find no physical menu here. Instead, bartenders dream up with concoctions on the fly based on each patrons taste. Boozehounds will also be well catered for at **28 HongKong Street** and **Jigger & Pony**, each serving expertly crafted concoctions with a twist. I'm a sucker for 28 HongKong Street's speakeasy vibe, barrel-aged Negronis and mean mac & cheese balls, while La Españita at Jigger & Pony always does the trick. If you're up for a Japanese-style experience, head to **Horse's Mouth** along Orchard Road (see page 62). It's a little hard-to-find, but that's part of the charm. (Hint: look for Uma Uma Ramen at #01-41 for the entrance to the bar.) For a view of the skyline, rooftop spot **Loof** is a decent bet. I favor their Asian-inspired options like the intriguing Singapore Sour (infinitely better than a Singapore Sling if you ask me) and Java Ginger Crush. Plus, you can pad your stomach with fab bar bites like chili crab dip with deep-fried mantou (buns), too.

---

28 HONGKONG STREET
28 HongKong Street S(059667) +65 6533 2001, 28hks.com

BAR STORIES
57A Haji Lane S(189250) +65 6298 0838, athousandtales.com

HORSE'S MOUTH
#B1-39 Forum The Shopping Mall, 583 Orchard Road S(238884)
+65 6235 1088, horsesmouthbar.com

JIGGER & PONY
101 Amoy Street S(069921) +65 6223 9101, jiggerandpony.com

LOOF
#03-07 Odeon Towers Extension Rooftop, 331 North Bridge Road S(188720)
+65 6338 8035, loof.com.sg

SINGAPORE AFTER DARK:
choice supper spots

Cure your midnight munchies

In case there was ever any doubt, eating truly is a national obsession in Singapore, and it doesn't stop even when it's time for bed. There are a ton of places to snag a late night bite when you're feeling peckish. From countless open-air neighborhood joints such as **Wen Dao Shi** (see page 127), serving up dim sum 24/7 in Geylang (see page 118), to **Outram Park Ya Hua Rou Gu Cha** ('meat bone tea'), a popular local haunt for comforting, slightly peppery bak kut teh (pork rib soup) that's usually open until 4am. Then there are eateries with special supper menus including **Fordham & Grand** (see page 28), don't miss their bang-for-your-buck $20 steak and fries, and **The Naked Finn** over in arts hub Gillman Barracks, offering scrumptious prawn vermicelli soup with secreto ibérico pork slices and a selection of grilled seafood. There's plenty of variety in our supper treats. Chow down on Mexican at **Pistola** on Club Street, perfectly placed for a quick burrito or taco on the go while bar hopping around Chinatown (see page 8).

FORDHAM & GRAND
43 Craig Road S(089681) +65 6221 3088, fng.com.sg

OUTRAM PARK YA HUA ROU GU CHA
#01-05/07 PSA Tanjong Pagar Complex, 7 Keppel Road S(089053)
+65 6222 9610

PISTOLA
93 Club Street S(069461) +65 6438 2185 / facebook.com/pistolasingapore

THE NAKED FINN
#01-13 Gillman Barracks, 41 Malan Road S(109454) +65 6694 0807
nakedfinn.com

WEN DAO SHI (126)
126 Sims Avenue S(387449) +65 6746 4757

PISTOLA

kampong glam

lavender

In my humble opinion, Kampong Glam is one of the most quaint, underappreciated areas in the city. Anchored by the impressive Sultan Mosque (see Religions of Singapore page 104), this conservation area is named after the many Gelam (Malaleuca) trees that grew in the Muslim Quarter in the past. The district, which extends to Arab Street and Haji Lane, hosts a number of F&B venues, carpet sellers and hip boutiques, as well as myriad shisha bars after-hours.

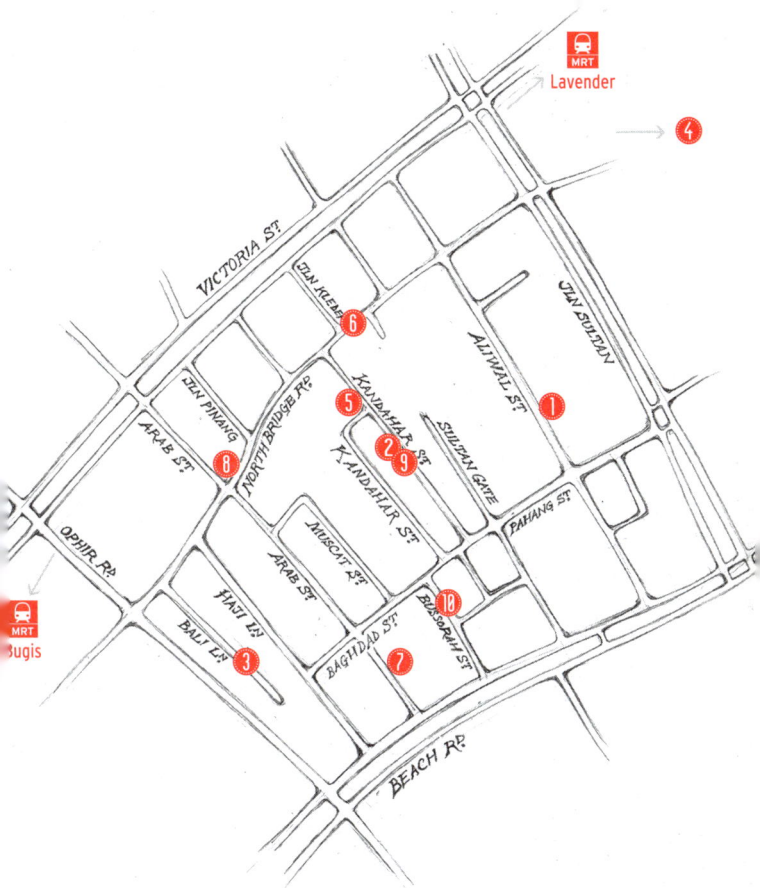

Map labels:
- Lavender (MRT)
- Bugis (MRT)
- VICTORIA ST
- JLN KLEDEK
- JLN SULTAN
- ALIWAL ST
- JLN PINANG
- NORTHBRIDGE RD
- KANDAHAR ST
- SULTAN GATE
- ARAB ST
- KANDAHAR ST
- MUSCAT ST
- PAHANG ST
- ARAB ST
- HAJI LN
- BALI LN
- BAGHDAD ST
- BUSSORAH ST
- BEACH RD
- OPHIR RD

1	A for Arbite	6	Roccoco Kent
2	Amir & Sons	7	Sifr Aromatics
3	Hounds of the Baskervilles	8	Singapore Zam Zam
4	Kilo (off map)	9	Tuckshop & Sundry Supplies
5	Maison Ikkoku	10	World Savage

A FOR ARBITE

Comfort food with craft beer pairings

#01-01 Aliwal Arts Centre, 28 Aliwal Street S(199918)
+65 8321 2252 / arbite.com.sg/home-a.php

Housed in Aliwal Arts Centre, a government-funded space for arts and performance groups , A for Arbite is the offshoot of chef-owner Marc Wee's Serangoon stalwart Arbite. A bit more hip yet still wallet-friendly, the menu features refined comfort food, each with recommended suds on tap or tea pairings. Go for the mini truffle beef burgers, tri-pepper spaghettini with soft shell crab or to end, a zingy lemon tart. It's also a great weekend brunch spot. Their pan-fried brandy and coffee-soaked brioche with gula melaka dip is killer.

AMIR & SONS

Fine Persian carpets

36 Kandahar Street S(198893) / +65 6734 9112
amirandsons.com

I'm a history nerd. I like to imagine sometimes that I was born in another century. A time filled with swashbuckling heroes brandishing curved scimitars; of caravans and camels weaving their way through the desert to the sound of lutes and drums. When I want to indulge my imagination, I visit Amir & Sons. Founded in 1921, this shop is a museum-like experience, and I've yet to find a more interesting carpet seller than its owner Mr. Amir. Although in his 70s, Mr. Amir personally takes visitors through the richly colored Persian rug collection that his father began nearly 100 years ago. Timeless and luxuriant, they seem almost too beautiful to step on.

HOUNDS OF THE BASKERVILLES

Edgy tattoo parlor and barbershop

24 Bali Lane S(189860) / +65 6299 1197
facebook.com/HoundsOfTheBaskervilles

Should you spot a hipster cruising down the street sporting Mad Men coiffed hair, a curly-q gelled 'stache and tats down his arms, said individual is likely en route to or from Hounds of the Baskervilles. Certainly the most edgy barber cum tattoo studio on the island, it's known for bringing in celeb guest tat artists and barbers from Australia, Japan and the States. Although they may crave a bad boy image, these guys are deeply involved in men's health awareness movement, Movember, so we think they're probably just a bunch of hair-snippin' do-gooder tattooists. Pop over and make up your own mind.

KILO

Soulful food in a low-key setting

2nd Floor 66 Kampong Bugis S(338987) / +65 6467 3987
kilokitchen.com

Every city has a couple of hidden, impossibly cool restaurants
and this is one of ours. Kilo is all the rage due to its brilliant
Japanese and Italian comfort cuisine, breezy setting and cool
sensibilities (kudos for the DJ station). Owners Javier Perez and
Sharon Lee want yours to be a communal meal, so plates are
prepared for sharing. I really like that aspect – bacon-wrapped
figs with creamy blue cheese just beg to be nibbled with friends.
Although Kilo is named for the nautical flag meaning "I want to
communicate with you," many haven't discovered it yet. So
don't wait.

MAISON IKKOKU

Café, designer menswear, and swanky bar

20 Kandahar Street S(198885) / +65 6294 0078 / maison-ikkoku.net

Some of the places I get to visit for work inspire me so much that I often times daydream about opening my own shop. Something involving stylish menwear, creative cocktails, and lots of exposed brick. In other words, something a lot like Maison Ikkoku. The owners have succeeded in pulling off a three-in-one concept involving a casual first floor café, a sharp-looking second floor menswear boutique, and a third-floor swanky after-hours cocktail bar. After snarfing down a delicious kong bak bao (steamed bun with stewed pork belly), wander upstairs for some of the most fashion-forward menswear in town. Finish on the third floor with an Old Fashioned on the rocks.

ROCCOCO KENT

Well-stocked vintage emporium

#02-02, 753 North Bridge Road (entrance on Jalan Kledek) S(198721)
+65 8522 8631 / roccocokent.com

In a city with a dearth of options for vintage vamps and retro fashionistas, Roccoco Kent is a true find. Toodle up the stairs to the second floor of a Kampong Glam shophouse and you will discover treasures aplenty. Most of the time when I shop for preloved goods I don't get my hopes up as there tends to be more chaff than wheat, but at Roccoco Kent I'm cooing over well-preserved leather bags and sustainable eco-jewelery. There's even a selection of home décor and collectibles to funk up your pad. Die-hard antiquarians should check in often to snag all the best swag.

SIFR AROMATICS

Custom perfumes and colognes

42 Arab Street S(199741) / **+65 6392 1966**

Step inside Sifr Aromatics and instantly you're whooshed away to a magical perfumed forest. Repurposed teak box shelves hold petite hand-blown perfume bottles that glisten like fiery jewels against Sifr's dark wooden planked floors and rich black walls. Owner Johari Kazura is a proud third generation perfume maker – that's his grandfather's framed portrait hanging on the wall. Set opposite the portrait is Johari's custom teak wood perfume bench, holding hundreds of individual natural oils that he melds into customized scents. Johari also sells a collection of ornate perfume bottles from the Czech Republic and antique silver atomizers from around the world.

SINGAPORE ZAM ZAM

Not your mama's murtabak

699 North Bridge Road S(198676) / **+65 6298 7011**

Prata is to Singapore what pizza is to NYC. It's cheap, hot, and delicious —
and usually available late at night after you've awoken the post-cocktail
hunger pains. So what could possibly make prata any better, you ask? Try
stuffing it with tender minced lamb or chicken, serve it bathed in golden
curry gravy, and call it murtabak. Zam Zam is a no-frills hole in the wall
that has been serving up this famous, best-in-town street food since
1908. After filling up, wander down Haji Lane for rose flavored hookah,
warm baklava and mint tea to wash it all down. A perfect night!

TUCKSHOP & SUNDRY SUPPLIES

Threads and accessories for the rugged

36a Kandahar Street S(198893) / +65 8181 2090
tuckshopsundrysupplies.com

There's something to be said for well-constructed products, whatever they are. At this menswear store, blokes can get kitted out from head-to-toe in solid-colored chambray or plaid flannel shirts, heavy duty rough-and-tumble jeans and jackets from labels like Rising Sun (Japan) and Red Cloud (China) and shoes from Oak Street Bootmakers. That's not all. Obbi Good Label, their in-house leather bags and accessories brand, rounds out the offerings. Each are handcrafted upstairs by owner and artisan Johnny Low. Low even holds leather workshops on select Saturdays for those keen on making their very own wallet or coin pouch. All you need to complete your James Dean look is a good dose of Layrite Deluxe Pomade for a high-shine, spiffy do.

WORLD SAVAGE

Vintage clothing and curios

70 Bussorah Street S(199483) / **+65 65368590** / **worldsavage.com**

An ode to the wanderer, to the curio collector, to those of us mad enough to walk down dark alleys in search of uncommon goods and lovingly cared for articles of yesteryear. An ode to the ladies who teach us true vintage from the fakery and to those who just don't care betwixt the two. An ode to those who leave their hair long, wear floppy boots, and swim where they're forbidden, to those who'd rather live the journey than read about it in a novel. An ode to loved vintage shirts and antique French cufflinks, to bone bead necklaces and feathered fedoras. An ode to World Savage and the lovable artists who run it. This should be on your don't-miss list just for the sheer wonderment of what you're bound to find inside.

religions of singapore

In good faith

♥

**ARMENIAN APOSTOLIC CHURCH OF
ST. GREGORY THE ILLUMINATOR**
60 Hill Street, armeniansinasia.org

CHURCH OF ST. TERESA
510 Kampong Bahru Road, stteresa.org.sg

KONG MENG SAN PHOR KARK SEE MONASTERY
88 Bright Hill Road, kmspks.org

MAGHAIN ABOTH SYNAGOGUE
24/26 Waterloo Street

MASJID SULTAN
3 Muscat Street, sultanmosque.org.sg

SAKYA MUNI BUDDHA GAYA TEMPLE
366 Race Course Road

SRI VEERAMAKALIAMMAN TEMPLE
141 Serangoon Road, sriveeramakaliamman.com

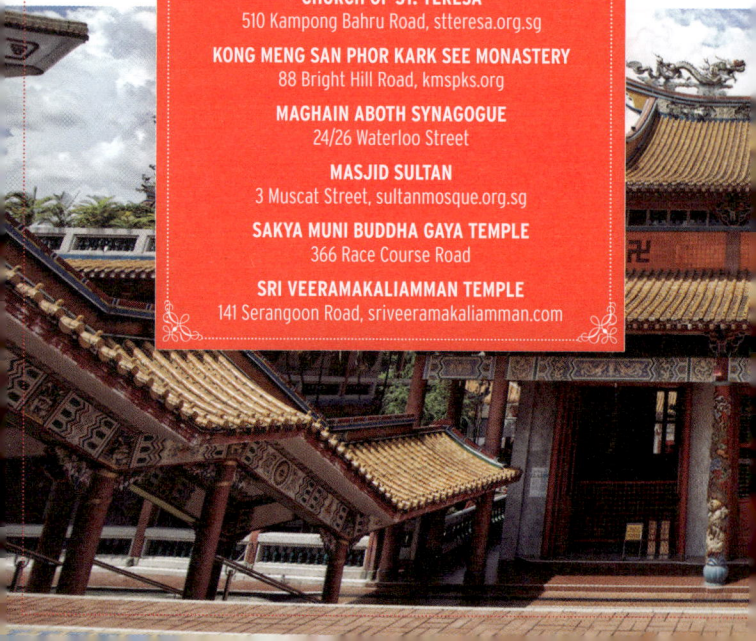

Singapore may be a small island, but the diversity of religions represented here never fails to amaze me. Most places of worship permit visitors to wander and some even provide tours, so be sure to fit in at least a few on your trip. For starters, check out the colorful **Sri Veeramakaliamman Temple** in Little India (see page 106). Also in the area is **Sakya Muni Buddha Gaya Temple** with its enormous golden Buddha. Singapore is also home to the oldest Jewish synagogue in Southeast Asia, **Maghain Aboth Synagogue**. Then there's **Masjid Sultan** (Sultan Mosque), a stunning mosque in Kampong Glam (see page 92). If you're up for some meditation off the beaten path, head to **Kong Meng San Phor Kark See Monastery** – a respite for monks since 1920. Lastly, not forgetting the Christians, there is the likes of **Church of St. Teresa** and the **Armenian Apostolic Church of St. Gregory the Illuminator**, the first Christian church built here back in 1835.

KONG MENG SAN PHOR KARK SEE MONASTERY

little india

jalan besar, mount emily

Undoubtedly one of the city's most colorful neighborhoods – and I do also mean that literally – Little India's full of fascinating sights, sounds and smells. You'll find everything from gorgeous temples (see Religions of Singapore page 104) to fantastic food to the 24-hour one-stop shop, Mustafa Centre. If you decide to head down on a Sunday, brace yourself for an overwhelmingly full-on experience as the streets are thronged with shoppers and foreign workers enjoying their much deserved weekly day off. Just a hop and skip away is Jalan Besar, an up-and-coming suburb with a growing number of cool eateries, bars and boutiques.

1 Carrie K. (off map)
2 Chye Seng Huat Hardware (off map)
3 CK Collection
4 Jewel Café + Bar (off map)
5 Khansama
6 Moghul Sweet Shop
7 Tyrwhitt General Company (off map)
8 Wild Rocket (off map)

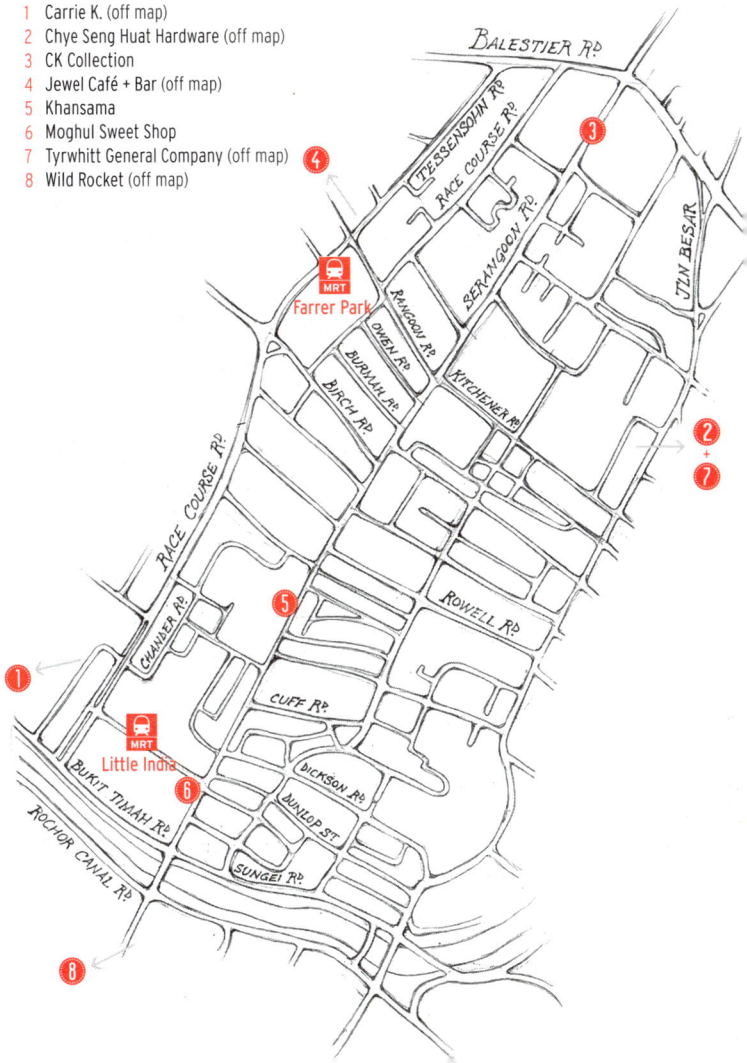

CARRIE K.

Eclectic artisanal jewelry

136 Bukit Timah Road S(229838)
+65 6735 4036 / carriekrocks.com

Carolyn Kan, or simply Carrie to those who know her
well, is the woman responsible for designing jewelry so exquisite
that I've had friends drag me away lest I give in to the very real
temptation of buying up everything in the store. She uses a range of
materials including rose gold, red coral and dual-sided colored leather
to produce unusual pieces with a decidedly modern appeal. I'm a fan
of the statement necklaces and cuffs from her Heavy Mettle and A
Beautiful Mess collections – sure fire ways to spice up any outfit. Plus,
this fashionable lady also happens to be one of the founders of Lolla's
Secret Supper, an underground dining club in Singapore.

CHYE SENG HUAT HARDWARE

Heavy duty java

150 Tyrwhitt Road S(207563) / **+65 6396 0609** / cshhcoffee.com

Calling all coffee geeks. Homegrown java hero Papa Palheta's joint pays homage to the many hardware stores in the area with its old school exterior. On display and for sale are toys such as siphons and Hario V60s. Sure, the place is mostly overrun with a skinny jeans-wearing hipster crowd (which makes for superb people watching), but the locally roasted goods in the form of long blacks and lattes keep us coming back. Those and their potent coffee beer that's a combo of the Terra Firma house blend and booze from local brewers Jungle Beer.

CK COLLECTION

Vintage lighting, fans, and collectables

586 Serangoon Road S(218200) / +65 6293 2301

Alas, there's no way – at least yet – to travel back in time. But it is possible to get a taste of those magical days at CK Collection. Owner CK has amassed a museum-worthy collection of vintage fans that date as far back as the 1800s. There are also antique lamps and art deco chandeliers aplenty that will delight anyone with a lighting fetish (guilty!). CK lives somewhere within this cluttered two-floor menagerie, but he's happy to show you around and tell you the interesting back stories of some of the pieces in his collection.

JEWEL CAFÉ & BAR

More than just a café

129 Rangoon Road S(218407) / +65 6298 9216
facebook.com/JewelCafeAndBar

It's hard to find a good cup of coffee and tasty grub in a casual setting in this town after hours so we were thankful when ex-banker Adrian Khong decided to set up a second outlet. (The original is in Shenton Way). The menu at this industrial chic neighborhood outfit packs a real punch with items like the satisfying OMG! Burger — USDA beef patty, bacon, cheddar, luncheon meat and a sunny side up. All cuppas are made with fresh-ground, single origin beans, with espresso-based drinks being double shots. An alternative to the usual suspects is the San Francisco, a cold brew concoction that takes 20 hours to make in a Kyoto dripper.

KHANSAMA

Stunning North Indian cuisine

166 Serangoon Road S(218050) / +65 6299 0300 / khansama.net

Here, you're spoiled for choice when it comes to Indian restaurants. Last time I looked there was something like four billion. The dirty little secret is that many of them are megachains, and many of the rest are just average. So let me point you towards my holy grail of Indian cuisine: Khansama. You may think you've savored tasty Indian cooking before, but prepare to be blown away. The food is outstanding partly because chefs are brought in directly from India to prepare owner Rakesh Sharma's secret recipes (they even go as far as whipping up fresh yogurt for their lassis).

MOGHUL SWEET SHOP

Authentic Indian desserts

Little India Arcade, 48 Serangoon Road S(217959) / +65 6392 5797

True story: As I alighted from my taxi outside Moghul Sweet Shop, I found myself squarely in the way of a, er... robust woman headed intently in my direction. I tried and failed to avoid a collision, and was bumped into oncoming traffic. To be fair, I don't think she saw me. I'm pretty sure her mind was elsewhere because when she saw the fresh sweets piled up at Moghul Sweet Shop (I kid you not) she yelled "THANK YOU GOD!" I also felt like shouting the same thing. Moghul has been serving authentic Indian sweet treats as long as anyone can remember. You'll be shouting too once you've tried them. Just don't kill anyone on your way.

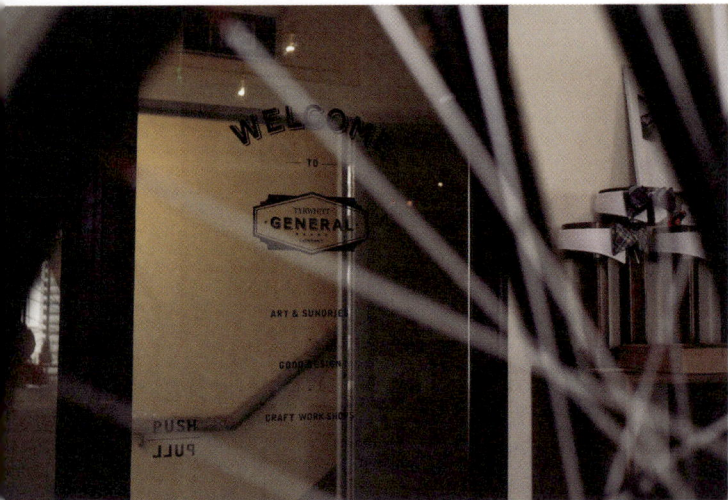

TYRWHITT GENERAL COMPANY

Handcrafted bags and accessories

150a Tyrwhitt Road S(207563) / tyrwhittgeneralcompany.com

If you ask me, there's a real charm about handmade products. Just looking at these beauts reminds me of a disappearing time when things weren't simply mass-produced in a factory. After all, what's not to love about beautiful pieces fashioned by passionate craftsmen? After you've gotten your caffeine fix at Chye Seng Huat Hardware (see page 109), climb up to the second floor and step into this tidy shop populated with ties from Singapore-based Crawford & Sons, cute canvas bags by NY label Out of Print and Oldman Handmade's suspenders and bow ties. The store also serves as a platform for budding designers and carries local jewelry brand By Invitation Only. Weekends even see events like silk screen workshops and pop-up concepts.

WILD ROCKET

Singaporean-inspired European cuisine

Hangout@Mt. Emily, 10a Upper Wilkie Road S(228119)
+65 6339 9448 / wildrocket.com.sg

After years of practicing law in Asia, I turned to my true passion – writing about food and shopping – the result of which you're holding in your hands. Another fellow lawyer turned foodie is Willin Low, owner and chef of Wild Rocket. This casual restaurant is nestled within the Hangout @ Mount Emily. Low purposefully blends traditional European fare with Singaporean flavors and spices, resulting in a unique hybrid you're not likely to find anywhere else. His laksa pesto linguini and black grouper with Cambodian amok are as unexpected as they are delicious. After dinner stroll across to Wild Oats, a bar housed in a restored colonial mansion.

asian desserts

Indulge your sweet tooth with these splendid treats

MEI HEONG YUEN'S MANGO AND STRAWBERRY SNOW ICE

MAJESTIC RESTAURANT'S CHILLED MANGO PUDDING WITH BLACK GLUTINOUS

I positively adore bakeries that exude that been-around-forever-no-nonsense vibe. The kind of place like **Rich & Good Cake Shop** in Kampong Glam (see page 92), a tiny bakery owned by Mrs. Lily Liu who whips up local delights such as Swiss rolls in flavors like kaya or durian, and an almond toast that is pure magic. Another old school bakeshop is **Galicier Confectionery** in Tiong Bahru (see page 36), which is responsible for some irresistible treats including onde onde (glutinous rice balls filled with gula melaka) and kueh dadar (a coconut-filled pandan-flavored pancake). Get your hands on tutu (steamed rice cake) from **Queensway Lau Tan Tutu Kueh** and be sure to try both the peanut and coconut. While you're in Chinatown (see page 8), beat the heat by digging into an epic shaved ice at **Mei Heong Yuen Dessert** in flavors like chendol, mango or strawberry. Also in the area is **Majestic Restaurant** (see page 13), perhaps better known for their savory Cantonese fare, but they also serve up some great, contemporary desserts. Their deep-fried durian ice cream is a stunner. If you're after something more traditionally Chinese, then pop by **Ah Chew Desserts** in Bugis (see page 74) for hot desserts including almond, walnut or sesame cream. As a bonus, it's usually open till 11pm (or later) most days.

AH CHEW DESSERTS
#01-11 Liang Seah Place, 1 Liang Seah Street S(189022) +65 6339 8198

GALICIER CONFECTIONERY
#01-39 Block 55 Tiong Bahru Road S(160055) +65 6324 1686

MAJESTIC RESTAURANT
Ground Floor New Majestic Hotel, 31-37 Bukit Pasoh Road S(089845) +65 6511 4718
restaurantmajestic.com

MEI HEONG YUEN DESSERT
67 Temple Street S(058611) +65 6221 1156, meiheongyuendessert.com.sg

QUEENSWAY LAU TAN TUTU KUEH
#B4-32 ION Food Hall, ION Orchard, 2 Orchard Turn S(238801)
facebook.com/queenswaytutukueh

RICH & GOOD CAKE SHOP
24 Kandahar Street S(198887) +65 6294 3324

east coast

geylang, joo chiat

———— ◆ ————

Despite Singapore's small geographical size,
there are those who still complain about how
far away the east side of the island is from the
central district. I think it's a myth perpetuated
by the Eastsiders themselves to keep us townies
at bay, so don't be fooled. East Coast is home to
neighborhoods like foodie enclave Joo Chiat –
historically a Straits Chinese stronghold – and
Geylang – perhaps more infamous for its red-
light district rep. There's also East Coast Park, a
popular weekend haunt for families, and of course,
Changi Village, a popular destination in itself with
locals for its food and shopping options.

MRT
Paya Lebar

MRT
Eunos

JOO CHIAT PLACE

BERYL RD.

JOO CHIAT LN.

KOON SENG RD.

JOO CHIAT RD.

PULASAN RD.

STILL RD.

CRANE RD.

DUNMAN RD.

HAIG LN.

CEYLON RD.

ONAN RD.

TEMBELING RD.

CHATELL CLOSE

HAIG AVE.

MARSHALL RD.

EAST COAST RD.

1 Chin Mee Chin Confectionery	5 Immigrants
2 Eng Seng Restaurant	6 Smokey's BBQ
3 Fu Lin Tou Fu Yuen (off map)	7 The Coastal Settlement (off map)
4 Jarrod Lim Design	8 Wen Dao Shi (126) (off map)

CHIN MEE CHIN CONFECTIONERY

Old school Singaporean brekkie joint

204 East Coast Road S(428903) / +65 6345 0419

Forget your eggs poached, scrambled or sunny side up. Breakfast in Singapore is all about hot kopi (coffee), soft-boiled eggs and buttery toast slathered thick with kaya (a sweet pandan and coconut jam). There are loads of eateries around town to satisfy your early morning cravings, but for a side order of nostalgia head to Chin Mee Chin Confectionery. You'll want to be an early bird though. This place is incredibly popular and its infamous raisin buns sell like hotcakes. Take it from me, they're worth waking up for, however late the previous night's bedtime hour.

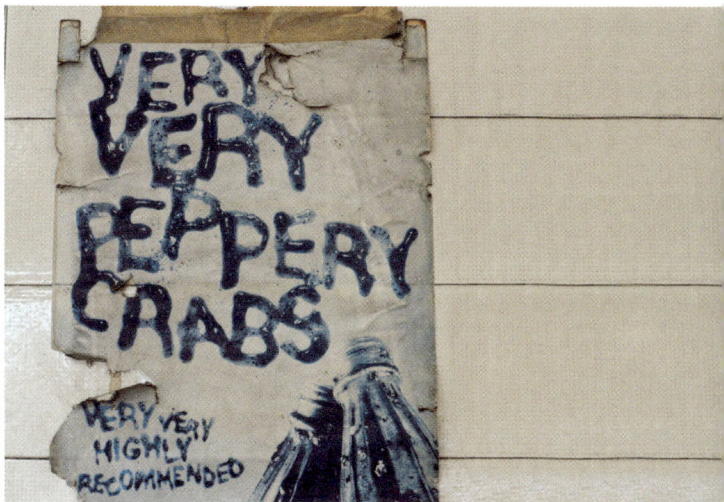

ENG SENG RESTAURANT

Local favorite for black pepper crabs

247-249 Joo Chiat Place S(427935) / +65 6440 5560

Chili crabs tend to pinch (geddit?) the limelight amongst tourists, but most Singaporeans I know prefer the black pepper variety. If you'd like to try the best of both, then visit what is arguably the most famous crab shack in town, Eng Seng Restaurant. Don't expect any frills though. Seriously — Oh, and be prepared to be in line by 5:30pm (or call ahead) to have any chance of nabbing a crab. Despite the difficulties, locals swear by it as the crustaceans here are always meaty and freshly caught. You'll want to wear dark clothing as eating these babies can get messy. But hey, that's half the fun, right?

FU LIN TOU FU YUEN

Sinfully crisp fried tofu and noodles

721 East Coast Road S(459070) / +65 6446 2363

For a proud male American Southerner, the following statement is a difficult admission. But here goes: I've grown to enjoy tofu. And after a visit to Fu Lin, you too will never look at bean curd the same way again. While most tofu restaurants steam their veggies and drown them in flavorless soup, Fu Lin fries them till they're crispy and smothers them in a heartstoppingly rich, savory chicken and mushroom sauce. Coupled with a side of homemade slippery noodles (that always seem to find their way onto my shirt), their yong tau foo never fails to satisfy. This is as basic as they come, but it's packed at all hours for a reason.

JARROD LIM DESIGN

Contemporary, clean-lined furniture

324 Joo Chiat Road S(427581) / +65 6440 0067 / jarrodlim.com

The first room I rented here was barely large enough to fit a double bed and a tiny workspace. And even though these days I've got a few more creature comforts, this writer's garret is by no means vast. In such confined space, it's important to have well-designed pieces that leave room for...well, living. Praise be for Jarrod Lim then, a master of clean furniture design in a style similar to Naoto Fukasawa, the celeb Japanese product designer from Muji. Functional but also playful, visit Jarrod's design studio to view and if you're lucky, meet with the man himself.

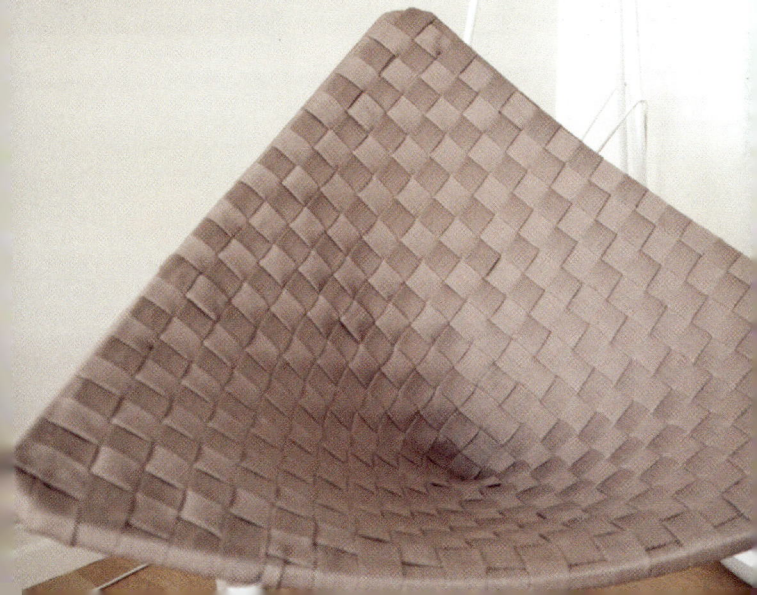

IMMIGRANTS

Peranakan grub with a twist

467 Joo Chiat Road S(427678) / +65 8511 7322
immigrants-gastrobar.com

Peranakan restaurants are a dime a dozen in this neck of the woods, but
if you're after something a little different, then this relaxed gastropub
is just the ticket. Look past the somewhat eclectic décor and settle in
for authentic, if modest (read: small) portions of Nyonya fare, alongside
a respectable choice of whiskeys and craft beers. I always order the
aromatic sambal chili buah keluak (black nut) fried rice – it's one of chef
Damian D'Silva's signatures, and a good match for most tipples. If you like
to spice things up, try the fiery charcoal-grilled Squid Bombs stuffed with
two kinds of chili. Explosive indeed.

SMOKEY'S BBQ

Authentic Southern American BBQ

73 Joo Chiat Place S(427790) / +65 6345 6914 / smokeysbbq.com.sg

Thanks to my Arkansan roots, I'm pretty particular about my barbecue, but Smokey's always hits the spot. I'm a very regular customer, purely in your service of course dear reader. The mouthwatering baby back ribs are so tender that the meat falls off the bone and come with a slurp-a-licious homemade BBQ sauce and coleslaw. To complete the all-American experience, choose from a range of microbrews imported from the States to wash it all down. Note that Arkansas flag on the wall – the chef also calls it home. Go hogs!

THE COASTAL SETTLEMENT

Casual family friendly hang-out near the beach

200 Netheravon Road S(508529) / +65 6475 0200
thecoastalsettlement.com

Singapore can feel a bit claustrophobic at times. Especially if you live or work right in the middle of the city. The weekends are a great time to escape the madness and find places off the beaten path. Enter one of my secret Sunday brunch spots to the rescue. This mecca of vintage mid-century furniture, Vespas and quirky artwork plates up homey comfort food in a forested laid-back atmosphere. It's perfect for the whole family as there's plenty of room for the kiddies to play outside in the grassy yard while the adults enjoy mimosas and buttery waffles in air-conditioned comfort inside.

WEN DAO SHI (126)

Excellent late-night dim sum

126 Sims Avenue S(387449) / +65 6746 4757

So you think the 126 in the name comes from the address of this place? So wrong. If you say the numbers out loud, one (wen) - two (dao) - six (shi), the direct Cantonese translation is either "welcome in the wealth" or, alternatively, "found a good place to eat." Them be good omens indeed. This Geylang legend serves rock-solid yummilicious dim sum 24 hours a day. The fried shallot-topped cheong fun is simply the best in town, and 126 rewrote the rulebook on creamy smooth century egg porridge. No wonder the long queues to get in, even late at night.

MINT MUSEUM OF TOYS
26 Seah Street S(188382) +65 6339 0660
emint.com

THE INTAN
69 Joo Chiat Terrace S(427231) +65 6440 1148
the-intan.com

quirky museums

Curios for the curious

Our island is home to a wonderful array of museums including the National Museum of Singapore, Asian Civilisations Museum and Singapore Art Museum; some offer discounted or even free admission in the evenings or on Fridays. But for something a little more quirky, there's the **Mint Museum of Toys**. Chang Yang Fa owns one of the finest toy collections in the world with over 100,000 pieces from more than 40 countries, many of them one of a kind. An off-the-beaten-track living museum is **The Intan** (meaning "rose cut diamond") in Joo Chiat (see page 118). The home of Alvin Yap, who began collecting antiques as a way to remember his family's heritage, is one of the best examples of a traditional Peranakan house in Southeast Asia. Tours are by appointment only, so remember to call ahead.